Nick Smethurst is a proud dad of two boys, Jake and Isaac.

Raised in Manchester, he is a proud northerner and likes to believe he has a good sense of humour; his friends would disagree!

Nick never intended on writing a book, let alone two books but the Covid lockdowns in the UK allowed him to start posting on social media about one of his passions: idioms/sayings/phrases and their origins.

Nick quickly realised he wasn't on his own with his fascination and after posting nearly 500 of these 'origin' stories, he has gained a large following of people who would get involved by posing new ones to him.

Dedications

Book 1 was dedicated to my children; this book is dedicated to parents – my amazing Mum and Stepdad, Pam and Brian Roscoe, who have always supported me in everything I do and my Dad, Mel Smethurst, who is the smartest guy I've ever met.

Acknowledgements

Special thanks to Peter Van Der Merwe for the amazing illustrations in this book.

Thank you to all the followers I have on LinkedIn; there are too many to name but without you all, I wouldn't have believed anyone else was interested in my obsession.

Nick Smethurst

AN IDIOT'S LOVE
OF IDIOMS 2

AUSTIN MACAULEY PUBLISHERS™

LONDON · CAMBRIDGE · NEW YORK · SHARJAH

A CIP catalogue record for this title is available from the British Library.

ISBN 9781398454781 (Paperback)
ISBN 9781035816552 (ePub e-book)

www.austinmacauley.com

First Published 2022
Austin Macauley Publishers Ltd®
1 Canada Square
Canary Wharf
London
E14 5AA

Table of Contents

"Chip Off the Old Block"

Meaning: someone who is very similar in character to their father or mother.

Origin: The earliest form of this phrase is 'chip of the same block'. The block in question would have been stone or wood. It dates back to at least 1621, when it appears in Bishop of Lincoln, Robert Sanderson's Sermons: "Am not I a child of the same Adam, a chip of the same block, with him?"

Shortly after this, we see a closer version to the modern one, swapping of for off, in John Milton's 'Remonstrant against Smectymnuus': "How well dost thou now appear to be a Chip of the old block."

It stayed 'of' rather than 'off' until the nineteenth century. The earliest exact reference I can find of today's phrase is in the Ohio newspaper The Athens Messenger, June 1870: "The children see their parents' double-dealings, see their want of integrity, and learn them to cheat. The child is too often a chip off the old block."

"A Good Egg"

Meaning: a likeable person.

Origin: The origin of this idiom is in its opposite and original idiom 'bad egg', first used in 1855 in Samuel A Hammett's novel 'Captain Priest generally' included the phrase. In the language of his class, the Perfect Bird generally turns out to be 'a bad egg'.

The analogy he draws is with an egg that on the outside may appear fresh, but when the shell is broken – it may be rotten inside. At the beginning of the twentieth century, students began reversing the phrase and describing decent people as a '*good egg*'.

"Fly Off the Handle"

Meaning: lose one's temper suddenly and unexpectedly.

Origin: Although the term 'fly off the handle' is relatively new compared to some other idioms, it is not a new concept. In Deuteronomy 19:5, 'God' mentions it in the Bible: "A man may go into the forest with his neighbour to cut wood, and as he swings his axe to fell a tree, the head may fly off and hit his neighbour and kill him."

Certainly, should this ever happen around someone, they would want to be the first to know it because it could hit them and kill them. The idiom in its current guise was first coined by American writer Thomas C. Haliburton's in *The Attaché, 1834*: "He flies right off the handle for nothing."

"Namby Pamby"

Meaning: lacking energy, strength or courage.

Origin: 'Namby Pamby' was a nickname invented in the eighteenth century by poet Henry Carey. He wrote a poem called *Namby Pamby*, 1725, to mock the English poet and playwright Ambrose Philips: "Namby-Pamby is your Guide, Albion's Joy, Hibernia's Pride."

Philips, a tutor to King George's grandchildren, gained notoriety for the sycophantic poems he wrote about his charges, often using babyish language such as 'eensy weesy', and his rival poet gave his own name the same treatment.

"Bad Books"

Meaning: in a state in which one is not liked or treated nicely.

Origin: In the Middle Ages, 'one's books' meant the esteem in which one was held by others. So, to be 'out of someone's books' meant you were no longer part of their life or of interest to them. This meaning is first recorded in *The Parlyament of Deuylles*, 1509 – "He is out of our books, and we out of his."

'Bad books' arrived on the scene much later and is first recorded in Perry's *History of the Church of England*, 1861: "The Arminians, who at that time were in his bad books."

"Goody Two Shoes"

Meaning: a person who always does everything right and always follows the rules, so much so that it becomes annoying.

Origin: The first 'Goody two shoes' is seen in print is in Charles Cotton's '*Voyage to Ireland in Burlesque*', 1670: "Why, then, Goody Two-shoes, what if it be? Hold you, if you can, your tittle-tattle," quote he.

The term became popular however with the publishing of the fable 'Goody Two-Shoes', Margery Meanwell whose nickname is 'Goody two shoes', goes through life with only one shoe. When a rich gentleman gives her a complete pair, she is so happy that she tells everyone that she has 'two shoes'. Later, Margery becomes a teacher and marries a rich widower. This earning of wealth serves as proof that her virtue has been rewarded, a popular theme in children's literature of the era. It is a variation of the story Cinderella.

Goody Two-Shoes was first published in 1765 and is thought to have been written by Irish author Oliver Goldsmith. The nursery rhyme book had very wide circulation for the time. The number of editions that have been published both in England and America is incredible and has appeared under numerous publishing houses in the UK and USA.

"In Spades"

Meaning: to a very high degree.

Origin: Spades is the highest-ranking suits in the game of Contract Bridge, a very popular pastime in the USA in the early twentieth century, which is when and where the phrase originated.

We have been 'calling a spade a spade' for many centuries, but the expression 'in spades' is a twentieth century US coinage. The term was often used before that in relation to card games, where Bridge contracts might be entered into in the minor suits of Clubs or Diamonds or, for the higher scores, 'in Hearts' or, best of all, 'in Spades'.

The figurative meaning, that is, the non-cards related meaning 'very greatly', isn't found before the 1920s. The first I can find of it in print is by American journalist and writer Damon Runyon when he used the expression that way in a piece for *Hearst's International* magazine, in October 1929: "I always hear the same thing about every bum on Broadway, male and female, including some I know are bums, in spades, right from taw."

"On the Wagon"

Meaning: abstaining from drinking alcoholic beverages.

Origin: When you 'fall off the wagon', you go back to drinking alcohol in large quantities after having abstained from it for a while. Nowadays, the expression is used to refer to the resumption of any bad activity – drugs, smoking, overeating, etc.

The 'wagon' in this American expression refers to the water wagons used to sprinkle water on the streets to keep the dust down. During the times of Prohibition in the nineteenth century, people often climbed onto these wagons and took an oath they would give up alcohol and drink only water. This gave rise to the expression 'to be on the water cart/wagon'; it was later shortened to 'on the wagon'.

When these individuals broke their pledge and started hitting the bottle again, they were said to have 'fallen off the wagon'.

"Time Flies"

Meaning: the phenomenon that time appears to pass more quickly when engaged in something you enjoy.

Origin: Though there is no definitive origin, this proverb is very old and has been traced back to Roman poet, Virgil (70–19BC) in his third book of the Georgics. In this, the Latin words: *'Fugit inreparabile tempus'* which translates to 'Time is flying never to return' can be seen.

It can be traced back in English to 1386 in Chaucer's 'Prologue to the Clerk's Tale' although there is no exact mention of time flies, the theory of time passing by quickly when one is enjoying themselves is explained.

One of the best-known uses of a similar phrase in English is in Shakespeare's work 'A lovers compliant', 1609: 'the swiftest hours, as they flew'.

We don't see 'Time flies' until the 1800s in English in its exact current format and the intensifier of 'when you're having fun' until much later. The theory of time moving quickly when one is enjoying oneself though really has its origin more than two millennia ago from the words of a Roman poet.

"Don't Cross a Black Cat"

Meaning: bad luck or bad omen.

Origin: In Middle Age Europe, a folklore spread about a man and his son who came across a black cat, which they began to toss rocks at. The injured cat ran into a woman's house who was suspected of being a witch and when the woman appeared limping and bruised the next day, people suspected that the cat must be the woman in disguise.

It is suggested that during this time, people started to see black cats as a sign of death and bad luck simply because of their black fur, just like ravens and crows.

The disturbing practice of prosecution of witches across Europe and eventually to the Salem Witch Trials began in 1692–3. Black cats whose owners were accused of witchcraft were associated with the Devil.

There were, however, plenty of black cat-lovers throughout history. Ancient Egyptians viewed black cats as divine and believed that gods lived within them. From the nineteenth century, the Irish believed that a black cat on your porch was good luck, and in Japan black cats are similarly revered as symbols of prosperity.

What we can say either way is, good or bad, black cats were revered as powerful creatures which clearly should not be crossed.

"Speak of the Devil"

Meaning: said when a person appears just after being mentioned.

Origin: 'Speak of the devil' is the short form of the English idiom 'Speak of the devil and he doth appear' or its alternative form 'speak of the devil and he shall appear'.

The phrase can be traced back to the seventeenth century and for a long time it implied the prohibition of mentioning the devil as superstition stated talking of the devil could bring his unwanted attention. The saying was a warning for centuries and was not used in the light-hearted manner it is today.

The first record of the saying in print is by Italian writer Giovanni Torriano in 'Piazza Universale', 1666: "The English say, Talk of the Devil, and he's presently at your elbow."

The saying stuck and is mentioned many times in print thereafter, even being recognised by the clergy. Richard Chenevix Trench, Dean of Westminster, 1856–63, wrote: "'Talk of the devil and he is bound to appear' contains a very needful warning against curiosity about evil."

In the nineteenth century, the threatening manner in which the saying was used began to fade and can be seen used more in line with the way it is used today.

"Haul Someone Over the Coals"

Meaning: to speak angrily to someone because they have done something you disapprove of.

Origin: The common theory for this idiom is of a practice in the UK in the sixteenth and seventeenth centuries. When someone was suspected of going against the church's preaching, one form of punishment was for these 'heretics' to be hauled over burning coals.

If they survived the ordeal, they would be declared innocent. Heretics were punished in the 15 and 1600s and this timeline fits well with the first example found in print. Henry VIII had made himself the head of the Church in 1534 and anyone at this time who did not have the same beliefs as him would be punished, some even executed.

According to the Oxford English Dictionary, the earliest printed record of the phrase can be traced back to 1565: "S. Augustine, that knewe best how to fetche an heretike ouer the coles," and is a direct reference to the torture.

By the early nineteenth century, the term had been transferred to more benign kinds of punishment, often signifying only a severe scolding, as in Byron's poem 'Beppo', 1818: "They'd haul o'er the coals."

"Mumbo Jumbo"

Meaning: a language or ritual causing or intended to cause confusion or bewilderment.

Origin: Mumbo Jumbo is an English word often cited by historians and etymologists as deriving from the Mandinka word 'Maamajomboo', which refers to a masked male dancer who takes part in religious ceremonies.

In the eighteenth century, Mumbo Jumbo referred to a West African god. 'Mungo Park's travel journal travels in the interior of Africa', written in 1795, describes 'Mumbo Jumbo' as a character, complete with 'masquerade habit', whom Mandinka males would dress up as in order to resolve domestic disputes.

The phrase appears more in line with its current meaning in Charles Dickens' 'Little Dorrit', originally published in serial form between 1855 and 1857: "He never dreamed of disputing their pretensions but did homage to the miserable Mumbo jumbo they paraded."

"Giving a Wide Berth"

Meaning: to avoid or stay away from someone or something.

Origin: This was originally a nautical term. We now think of a ship's berth as the place where the ship is moored. Before that though it meant 'a place where there is sea room to moor a ship'. This derives in turn from the probable derivation of the word berth, that is, 'bearing off'. When sailors were warned to keep a wide bearing off something, they were being told to make sure to maintain enough sea room from it.

An early example comes from Captain John Smith in '*Accidental Young Seamen*', 1626: "Watch bee vigilant to keepe your berth to windward."

Berth came to be adopted more widely into the language, just meaning a safe distance from anything. There are several such figurative uses of it in the seventeenth and eighteenth centuries. We have to wait until 1829 for Sir Walter Scott's '*Letters on demonology and witchcraft*' for 'a wide berth' though: "Giving the apparent phantom what seamen call a wide berth."

"A Wolf in Sheep's Clothing"

Meaning: a person or thing that appears friendly or harmless but is really hostile.

Origin: The warning that you can't necessarily trust someone who appears kind and friendly on the outside is centuries old, dating back to the bible.

This is first seen in print in the King James Version of the Bible, 1611, and has this passage in Matthew 7:15: "Beware of false prophets, which come to you in sheep's clothing, but inwardly they are ravening wolves."

"All Systems Go"

Meaning: a state of readiness for immediate action.

Origin: In 1961, Alan Shephard was the first ever American astronaut in space as part of the 'Freedom 7' spacecraft mission. Shephard was broadcast to the listening American public and his quote onboard the ship was: "Cabin pressure go, fuel systems go, oxygen go, all systems go."

This was the first time we hear the phrase 'All systems go' used and it spread around the English-speaking world rapidly.

It started to be used figuratively in many other contexts, for example just one year later where it is seen in print first in the 'Birmingham Daily Post', 1962: "Then suddenly, just after half-time, it was 'all systems go' for Tottenham."

"Off the Cuff"

Meaning: without preparation or spur of the moment.

Origin: This saying derives from cinema; it is said that actors and movie directors would literally write their lines on the cuffs of their shirts in order to remember them 'in the moment'.

The earliest example of this in print is from the New York magazine, 'The film daily', reporting on Jack Cohn (Co-founder and producer at Columbia pictures) in March 1928: "Somebody said Jack Cohn had 'stymied' and Jack wrote it on his cuff as a good title for a future Columbia release." This example is where Jack had wrote something down at the Rockville Country Golf Tournament in order to remember it later.

The saying was seen several times in print after this and has since come to mean anything that is dealt with without preparation not just lines in movies. The first example of it being used in its current format is just months later again in 'The film daily' in October 1928: "The supermen of the megaphone will no longer 'shoots 'em off the cuff' after ostentatiously destroying the scenario."

"Spur of the Moment"

Meaning: done without planning in advance or impulsive.

Origin: The 'spur' referenced in 'spur of the moment' are the spurs used to urge a horse forward at speed. Spurs have been used this way for Millenia, the first known use of spurs is by Celts in the La tene period which began 500BC.

The first time we see spurs being used in a figurative way to mean 'act immediately' in English is in 1525 when English translator John Bourchier translates French writer Jean Froissart's 'The gauntoyse fledde out of dan by night' thought to be written around 1400. The translation eludes to an earlier saying, "Ride on the spurs."

The first example of the saying as it is now can be seen in the 'Jackson's Oxford Journal', 1784: "The idea of Lord Ferrers, though probably set forward on the spur of the moment, looks at first as if it would lead to something worth attending."

"Jumping the Gun"

Meaning: act before the proper or appropriate time.

Origin: The origin of 'Jump the gun' or 'Jumping the gun' comes from Track and field races and originates in the USA. The term was originally 'Beat the Pistol' and the first example of this in print is in Crowther and Ruhl's 'Rowing and Track Athletics, 1905: "Beating the pistol was one of the tricks which less sportsmanlike runners constantly practised."

The earliest figurative example in print for the saying as it is today, 'jump the gun', is found in 'The Iowa Homestead', 1921: "Give the pigs a good start; jump the gun, so to speak, and get them on a grain ration before weaning time."

In 1942 the term is recognised as slang in 'The American Thesaurus of Slang' and is described as 'to make a false start'.

The term started to be used regularly as being overzealous in any situation around the 1950s.

"Between the Devil and the Deep Blue Sea"

Meaning: in difficulty, faced with two dangerous alternatives.

Origin: The phrase was originally 'Between the Devil and the deep sea'. The sea turned blue much later and the phrase became well-known via the title of a popular song 'Between the Devil and the Deep Blue Sea', written by Ted Koehler and Harold Arlen, and recorded by Cab Calloway in 1931.

Greek mythology points towards an earlier version of the idea of being caught between evil and the sea. Homer's Odyssey refers to Odysseus being caught between Scylla (a six-headed monster) and Charybdis (a whirlpool).

We can't be sure if this was the origin of the saying however, but we can be sure the saying is 400 years old at least as the first recorded citation of 'the Devil and the deep sea' in print is in Robert Monro's 'His expedition with the worthy Scots regiment called Mac-keyes', 1637: "I, with my partie, did lie on our poste, as betwixt the 31 evil and the deep sea."

"Take It with a Pinch/Grain of Salt"

Meaning: to regard something as exaggerated.

Origin: The first use of this phrase is very old indeed but was not originally meant in the 'tongue in cheek' way we use it today. The original usage was actually thought to be a perceived antidote to poison.

An English translation of the ancient Roman author, Pliny the Elder's work in 77AD: "Take two dried walnuts, two figs and twenty leaves of rue, pound them all together, with the addition of a grain of salt, if a person takes this mixture fasting, he will be proof against all poisons for that day."

We don't see the words in English until much later in John Trapp's Commentary on the Old and New Testaments, 1647: "This is to be taken with a grain of salt."

The American use of the phrase is with a 'grain of salt' whereas in the UK, it is a 'pinch of salt' is more common. The figurative usage seems to be more recent and the first examples of both can be seen in the twentieth century, 1908 is the earliest example of 'grain' being used and 1948 'pinch'.

What we can say is the figurative usage must have come from the watering down effect salt was thought to make something less serious.

"The Cut of One's Jib"

Meaning: one's general appearance or personality.

Origin: Sir Walter Scott brought this phrase into common use in in 'St Ronan's Well', 1824: "If she disliked what the sailor calls the cut of their jib."

The jib of a sailing ship is a triangular sail set between the fore-topmast head and the jib boom. Some ships had more than one jib sail. Each country had its own style of sail and so the nationality of a sailing ship, and a sailor's consequent opinion of it, could be determined from the jib.

'Not liking the cut of someone's jib', which is usually the context it is commonly used in, is stating you don't like the way they look in effect because of something recognisable about them, like a jib can be recognised on a ship.

"Green-Eyed Monster"

Meaning: jealousy.

Origin: The theory behind this idiom is thought to be that green is associated with illness, people's skin is known to take a yellow or green tinge when they are seriously ill.

Shakespeare was the first to use a very similar term where it is believed the idiom originated in *'The Merchant of Venice', 1596*: "And shuddering fear, and green-eyed jealousy! O love, be moderate."

Shakespeare is also the first to write the exact term 'green eyed monster' in his most famous play about jealousy, 'Othello', 1604: "O, beware, my lord, of jealousy. It is the green-eyed monster which doth mock the meat it feeds on."

"In the Limelight"

Meaning: at the centre of public attention or notoriety.

Origin: The 'lime' in limelight has nothing to do with the green citrus fruit but rather with a chemical compound, calcium oxide, also known as quicklime. Heating a piece of 'lime' in a flame of burning oxygen and hydrogen produces an intense white light.

The effect was discovered in the 1820s by Goldsworthy Gurney and the application of the process to create a bright light was developed by Thomas Drummond around 1825. It was widely used in nineteenth century theatres to illuminate the stage and was first used in a public theatre at Covent Garden in London in 1837.

The figurative use didn't come along until a while after and the first example in print can be found in 'The New York Times', 1902: "William S. Devery was in the limelight last evening. Tens of thousands of people of the district crowded the streets in the neighbourhood and shouted the name of the ex-Chief of Police of New York."

"In the Buff"

Meaning: naked.

Origin: A buff-coat was a light browny/yellow leather tunic worn by English soldiers between the late sixteenth century and the late seventeenth century. The original meaning of 'in the buff' was simply to be in this uniform coat.

Shakespeare makes reference to this in the play 'The Comedy of Errors', 1590: "I know not at whose suit he is arrested well, but he's in a suit of buff which 'rested him, that can I tell."

The current meaning of 'in the buff' is simply an allusion to the pale skin coloured coat and this was first recorded by Thomas Dekker, in his work 'Satiro-mastix or the untrussing of the humorous poet', 1602: "No, come my little Cub, doe not scorne mee because I goe in Stag, in Buffe, heer's veluet too." 'In Stag' mentioned here was a term used in the 1600s as another term for naked.

"In Stitches"

Meaning: laughing uncontrollably.

Origin: According to the Oxford English dictionary, as early as the year 1000 a 'stitch' was known as a stabbing pain in the side. It is believed the phrase 'in stitches' is reference to laughing so hard that you are in pain.

The first reference of the phrase seen in print is in Shakespeare's 'Twelfth Night', 1602: "If you desire the spleen, and will laugh yourself into stitches, follow me."

Despite this early example it is not seen again in print until 300 years later in 'The Lowell Sun', 1914: "There's a new face among the members in Ben Loring, a natural-born comedian, who seems to have no difficulty whatever in keeping his audience in stitches of laughter and glee."

The phrase must have been commonly in use by the early twentieth century for it to be understood in print, but the origin, as with so many other modern-day phrases, lies with Shakespeare.

"Push the Boat Out"

Meaning: a large celebration or expense.

Origin: For centuries, boats have been made that are too large for an individual to move. Helping a seaman to push a boat out was seen as an act of generosity and this is where the phrase is thought to have originated.

We first see the phrase used in the context of being generous in print in Edward Fraser and John Gibbons' 'Soldier and Sailor Words and Phrases', 1925: "Push the boat out, to stand treat."

Shortly after the phrase became used in UK nautical circles to mean 'buy a round of drinks' in the 1930s and the first example of this in print is in J. Curtis' 'You're in Racket', 1937:

"This bloke you're meeting up the Old Jacket and Vest to-night, let him push the boat out."

The term 'push the boat out' is now used more generally and has come to mean making a purchase that is rather beyond what one can afford.

"My Neck of the Woods"

Meaning: the place or area where someone lives.

Origin: The phrase is thought to come from the sense of 'neck' as a strip of land.

This one is not definitive and there are a few theories behind it. In Britain, a 'neck' can refer to land with water on both sides however early Americans used it to mean a settlement in the woods.

In Bill Bryson's 'Made in America', the claim is made that the origin of 'neck' is the Algonquian (native American language) word 'naiack' meaning 'point' or 'corner'.

The final theory is that the phrase 'my neck' could derive from the German phrase '*meine ecke*' which would translate to 'my corner'.

What we can say definitively is that the phrase is first seen in print in M. Schele de Vere's book 'Americanisms', 1839: "He will find his neighbourhood designated as a neck of the woods."

"At the Drop of a Hat"

Meaning: immediately or without delay.

Origin: the phrase 'at the drop of a hat' is thought to originate in the early nineteenth century. At this time, it was very common to drop or sweep a hat in a rapid downward motion to signal the beginning of a fight or race.

The term began to be used in a more figurative way, meaning to act quickly, around the 1830s and the first recorded example in print of this can be seen in a registered debate of American congress in relation to a hearing on bankruptcy law in 1837: "They could agree in the twinkling of the eye, at the drop of the hat, at the crook of a finger."

"Fingers Crossed"

Meaning: a hand gesture commonly used to wish for luck.

Origin: The saying comes from the common gesture which traces back to the early centuries of the Christian Church, and likely earlier. Christians would cross their fingers to invoke the power associated with Christ's cross.

The phrase 'Fingers crossed' as oppose to the gesture is much more modern and can first be seen in print in 'A Provincial Glossary' by Francis Grose, 1787: "Keep one's fingers crossed until one sees a dog to avert the bad luck attracted by walking under a ladder."

Interestingly in Vietnam, the gesture is considered rude and is the equivalent of the middle finger and in Sweden and German speaking countries the gesture is a sign of lying.

"Keen as Mustard"

Meaning: very enthusiastic.

Origin: The most common theory is that the heat of mustard is used figuratively in this phrase to display someone's energetic behaviour. The logic of this can be seen in the slightly earlier saying, 'As hot as mustard'.

Although there is no definitive origin for this phrase what we can say for certain is the saying with 'hot' has been around from at least the late seventeenth century. We see the phrase first in print in its current guise in F. Smith's 'Clod-pate's Ghost', 1679: "You shall see a man as hot as Mustard against Plot and Plotters."

Although the words 'Keen as mustard' can be seen as early as 1672 in print in William Walkers 'Phrases of the English and Latin tongue', 'hot' was more readily used than 'keen' at this point. The saying with 'Keen' is thought to have been popularised by the brand 'Keen's Mustard' which started to be manufactured in 1742 in the UK.

"Loose Cannon"

Meaning: an unpredictable or uncontrolled person.

Origin: Between the seventeenth and nineteenth centuries, warships used cannons as their primary offensive weapons. The term 'loose cannon' comes from the idea a cannon that had become free of its restraints would be able to role dangerously about the deck.

Although this is the likely origin, there is no evidence that this happened in the era the cannons were being used. The first time we see the term in print is in Henry Kingsley's novel 'Number seventeen', 1875: "At once, of course, the ship was in the trough of the sea, a more fearfully dangerous engine of destruction than Mr Victor Hugo's celebrated loose cannon."

Shortly after, the term 'loose cannon' started to be used figuratively for anything, usually people, that was out of control. The first time we see this is in reference to the trouble that could be caused within the votes in an election in 'The Galveston Daily News', 1889: "It would in no event become, as Mr Grady once said, a loose cannon in a storm-tossed ship."

"Having a Chip on One's Shoulder"

Meaning: to have an angry or unpleasant attitude.

Origin: The common theory for the origin of this phrase is based on the nineteenth century U.S. practice of spoiling for a fight by carrying a chip of wood on one's shoulder, daring others to knock it off.

The first time we see this in print is in James Kirke Paulding's 'Letters from the South', 1817: "This, it seems, is equivalent to throwing the glove in days of yore, or to the boyish custom of knocking a chip off the shoulder."

There is another theory that the phrase has nautical origins and indeed we do see 'chips on shoulders' mentioned earlier in reference to sailors physically carrying wood and surplus 'chips' that could be kept by the sailors for firewood. This however has a completely different meaning which is why the popular theory of someone being 'cocky' comes from the American version where one may be spoiling for a fight.

"Hold Your Horses"

Meaning: wait a moment.

Origin: The first reference to this saying is from the translated work of the ancient Roman author, Homer. In book 23 of the Iliad, roughly 800BC, he wrote: 'Hold your horses' when referring to Antilochus driving like a maniac in a chariot race that Achilles initiates in the funeral games for Patroclus. This was meant literally and it is uncertain if this citation was transformed in to the figurative way we use it today.

Around the 1600s in the United Kingdom, one punishment for law breakers would be to trample them to death with horses. The person in charge would 'Hold their horses' whilst the law breaker was restrained and tied to a piece of wood on the ground.

The figurative use that doesn't actually involve physically restraining horses comes much later and seems to have its origins in America. The first printed usage of it this way can be found in a newspaper in Picayune, New Orleans, 1844: "Oh, hold your horses, Squire. There's no use getting riled."

"A Lightbulb Moment"

Meaning: a moment of sudden realisation, enlightenment or inspiration.

Origin: The invention of the lightbulb was so revolutionary that for over a century, it has symbolised having an idea. The phrase 'Lightbulb moment' is directly related to Thomas Edison's invention of the lightbulb in 1879.

The symbolism, where a lightbulb is shown above one's head to mean 'idea' was first expressed in Pat Sullivan and Otto Messmer's American comic strip 'Felix the Cat', 1919. Shortly after this, we see lightbulbs being used in other media.

The saying 'The light bulb moment' has no definitive origin other than it is directly related to Edison's invention and is symbolised by early twentieth century comic strips.

"The Penny Dropped"

Meaning: someone finally understands something after not understanding it for a time.

Origin: The Oxford English Dictionary states that this phrase originated by way of allusion to the mechanism of penny-in-the-slot machines. People would try and cheat the machine by putting paper in the machines and only the noise of an actual penny dropping into the machine would make the right and recognisable sound.

The first time we see the figurative use of the phrase with the 'now I understand' meaning, is from The Daily Mirror, 1939: "And then the penny dropped, and I saw his meaning."

"Something Fishy Is Going On"

Meaning: something of doubtful character or suspicious.

Origin: This phrase originates in the 1800s. Unlike today, there was no 'best by' date attached to the fish sold and fish was usually purchased at a fish market. The only way one would know that the fish being sold was fresh was if it did not stink. If the fish had a foul odour, then it may mean that the fishmonger was being dishonest because only stale fish had an odour.

The first time we see 'fishy' being used in the 'suspicious' context in print is in J.G Holland's 'Everyday topics', 1876: "Fish is good but fishy is always bad." This example is literal, however just four years later in 1880, we see it in print being used figuratively in James Payne's 'Confidential Agent': "His French is very fishy."

"Change Tack"

Meaning: changing direction or course of action.

Origin: The phrase 'change tack' came into use as an idiom in the 18th Century although 'tack' being used in a directional sense comes much earlier and is derived from a nautical term. In sailing, changing tack or tacking, is a sailing manoeuvre by which a sailing vessel, whose desired course is into the wind, turns its bow towards the wind propelling the boat.

We see 'tack' used many times in print in reference to sailing in the 1600s mentioning the 'tack' that holds the ropes for the sails on a boat. 'Tack' is mentioned in print for the first time in a directional sense in 1679 in an anonymous journal: "Now the Court was certainly making a tack towards the Coast of Italy."

We then see the term 'Change tack' first used in print in Jacques-Raymond Grenier's 'The Art of War at Sea', 1788: "We will be able to observe the manoeuvres of the enemy, in order to change tack and form themselves in Order of Battle on the opposite board."

The term is now used figuratively in any situation where there is a change of plan or direction.

"Piggy Back"

Meaning: carrying someone on your back or shoulders.

Origin: This term has nothing to do with pigs and over the centuries the word has morphed from the original saying, 'pick a pack' or 'back', referring to a pack that could be carried on the back like todays back packs. When someone was carried on another's back it was referred to as a 'pick a pack' or 'back'.

The first printed version of the term in this way is in James Calfhill's 'An aunswere to treatise of the crosse', 1565: "Whereto we may be caried a pickbacke on a horse."

We don't see the term with 'pigs' in until 1736 in Robert Ainsworth's 'Thesaurus linguae *Latinae compendiarius*': "Back to carry on pig back." It is thought, as with many such terms that the words have been changed over the two centuries to be more recognisable and fun as normally children are the benefactors of the 'piggyback' and it is an alternative play on words.

We finally see the full transformation as we see it today first in print In Baynard Rush Hall's 'The new purchase', 1843: "Meanwhile, two thus doing piggy-back in reverse order, had gradually advanced to the door."

"We'll Cross That Bridge When We Come to It"

Meaning: something said when you do not intend to worry about a possible problem now but will deal with it if or when it happens.

Origin: Even though the origin of the phrase is not known, it has been used since well before the 1800s where the crossing of bridges was quite a literal thing with long travels being done either on foot or horseback.

The bridge could not be crossed before it actually came up and moreover, the crossing of bridges was considered a risky matter because the reliability of faraway bridges was not guaranteed. Crossing a bridge related to a huge problem which is, in today's terms used as a synonym of solving problems. Although life is not at stake in the usage of the phrase today, it used to be when people were discussing about actually crossing shaky bridges.

The first recorded use of the idiom can be found in Henry Wadsworth Longfellow's 'The Golden Legend', 1851: "Don't cross the bridge till you come to it, is a proverb old and of excellent wit."

"Winging It"

Meaning: to do or try to do something without much practice or preparation.

Origin: This expression comes from the theatre, where it alludes to an actor studying their part in the wings, which are the areas to either side of the stage, because they have been suddenly called on to replace another. Another popular idiom related to this is the fact that stage actors 'wait in the wings' at the side of the stage until it's time for them to play their part in the drama.

This phrase dates from the late nineteenth century and the verb 'to wing' was defined in 'Stage magazine', 1885: "To wing indicates the capacity to play a role without knowing the text."

The phrase 'winging it' is first seen in print in Philip Godfrey's 'Back-stage: a survey of the contemporary English theatre from behind the scenes', 1933: "He must give a performance by 'winging it', that is, by refreshing his memory for each scene in the wings before he goes on to play it." The phrase must have been well-established before then though for it to be understood in this script.

"Over a Barrel"

Meaning: in a helpless position or at someone's mercy.

Origin: This is believed to be a term of nautical origin and derives from the practice of hanging a drowned, usually unconscious person over a barrel to clear their lungs of water. The fate of the 'patient' was determined solely by the actions of those administering the treatment and therefore at their mercy.

The term 'over a barrel', in the 'at someone else's mercy' meaning, is also used as people would receive punishment whilst tied 'over a barrel' and this is where it is first seen in print referring to a college initiation ceremony in newspaper 'The Daily Republican', 1886: "He was bound hand and foot and rolled over a barrel."

The saying began to be used more figuratively soon after, meaning 'being in trouble', in general and the first example seen in print is in 'The Seattle Post-Intelligencer', 1893: "The good, true, loving wife she appeared to be, being, to use a slang phrase 'over a barrel'."

"Use Your Loaf"

Meaning: use one's common sense.

Origin: The phrase to use your loaf is derived from the cockney rhyming slang for head which is loaf of bread. This is first seen in the early twentieth century.

This use of loaf is first recorded in Edward Fraser and John Gibbons' 'Soldier and Sailor Words and Phrases', 1925: "Duck your loaf, keep your head below the parapet."

"A Level Playing Field"

Meaning: a situation in which everyone has a fair and equal chance of succeeding.

Origin: This phrase alludes to the fairness required in field games where a slope would clearly be an advantage for one side.

Figuratively, it has been used since the late twentieth century, with the oldest recorded version found being in the 'Tyrone Daily Herald', 1977: "Our philosophy is that we have no problem competing with the mutual savings banks if they start from the level playing field."

It is thought this saying comes from another American phrase, 'on the level', meaning above board and fair. This is first recorded in George Burnham's 'Memoirs of the United States Secret Service', 1872: "On the level, meeting a man with honourable intentions."

"Knowing One's Onions"

Meaning: someone experienced in something or that knows a lot about a particular subject.

Origin: Although there is no definitive origin for this saying, one popular theory is that the 'onion' in 'Know your onions' is English grammarian Charles Talbut Onions, who was an editor of the Oxford English Dictionary from 1895–1966 and was an expert etymologist and he certainly 'knew his onions' where words were concerned.

This popular theory cannot be correct however, as all the early records of this saying are American, not English. We see it mentioned numerous times in American print in the early twentieth century and not until the mid-twentieth century in England. The earliest example found in print is from 'The Philadelphia Inquirer', 1898: "You must know your onion to get your money on right."

Why onions? Nobody knows for certain, and the reason has been lost to the sands of time. A popular theory is that 'onion' is a shortened version of 'onion rings', rhyming slang for 'things', as in they know things, but again there is no definitive proof of this. What we can say is that the saying is over 100 years old and has its roots (pun intended!) in America.

"Dropped a Clanger"

Meaning: to make a very bad or embarrassing mistake.

Origin: The noun clanger is used only in this phrase, the image is of something dropping with a clang, which underlines the conspicuous nature of a mistake.

This phrase seems to have originated in British Army slang during or immediately after the Second World War, the earliest instance found is from 'Beeze Up Your English', published in London paper, the 'Daily Herald', 1945: "It is so easy for the innocent civilian to drop a clanger (make a mistake)."

Later in 1945, several Canadian and U.S. newspapers published an article distributed by The Canadian Press, apparently inspired by the British article, 'The Ottawa Journal' used this used the same phrase and it seems to have taken hold since then.

The phrase must have already been commonly understood in British army circles for it to be in print but certainly it seems to have been defined somewhere in the early 1940s.

"Another String to One's Bow"

Meaning: more than one ability or thing they can use if the first one they try is not successful.

Origin: This term comes from the custom of archers carrying a reserve string. It first appeared in English in the mid-fifteenth century, and in 1546 it was in John Heywood's collected proverbs book 'A dialogue *conteinyng the number in effect of all the Prouerbes in the Englishe tongue*'.

Bowstrings in the 'bow and arrow' or combat sense of the word, would often lose effectiveness on their way to the battlefield, either because of ordinary wear and tear, or because of unusual, but not unforeseen events like rain. Since 'bowstrings' were the most easily replaced part of a bow, archers would carry several of them at one time, to make sure that at least one was working at maximum efficiency.

"The Sands of Time"

Meaning: the passing of time.

Origin: The most common theory is that the sands of time is reference to the hourglass, a device used to measure time for many centuries. The earliest documented example of the hourglass is as early as the eighth century and was crafted by a Frankish monk named Liutprand who served at the cathedral in Chartres, France.

It was not until the fourteenth century that the hourglass was seen commonly however with the next firm evidence being a painting from 1338 named 'Allegory of Good Government' by Ambrogio Lorenzetti.

The phrase 'The sands of time' however is not seen until much more recently in print and the first example found is in Henry Wadsworth Longfellow's 'A psalm of life', 1839: "Lives of great men all remind us we can make our lives sublime. And, departing, leave behind us footprints on the sands of time."

"Cloud Nine"

Meaning: a feeling of well-being or elation.

Origin: Elation hasn't always been about cloud nine, in fact before we see cloud nine mentioned as the blissful state we see it today, we see happiness found in cloud eight. We also see seven mentioned around the same time as we see 'nine' being described as the happy state we understand it to be.

Cloud eight comes first in Albin Pollock's directory of slang, 'The Underworld Speaks', 1935: "Cloud eight, befuddled on account of drinking too much liquor."

'Cloud nine' comes a little later and the first example in print is found in 'The Oxnard Press-Courier' 1946: "I think he has thought of everything, unless the authorities pull something new on him out of cloud nine."

Around the same period, we find cloud seven in 'The San Mateo Times', 1952: "Mantovani's skilled use of reeds and strings puts this disc way up on Cloud Seven."

Since the 1980s, 'cloud nine' has become predominant. The most common theory for why 'cloud nine' won through is thought to be influenced by its use in popular music. The Temptations' (1969), George Harrison (1987) and Bryan Adams (1999) all had albums or songs with the name 'cloud nine'.

Why nine in the first place? The most common theory for this is thought to be found in the 1895 'International cloud atlas'. Cloud nine is listed as cumulonimbus, the largest and puffiest of all the clouds.

"Catch 22"

Meaning: a paradoxical situation from which an individual cannot escape because of contradictory rules or limitations.

Origin: This one has a definitive origin, and it comes from Joseph Heller's 1961 novel 'Catch-22', which describes absurd bureaucratic constraints on soldiers in World War II.

The term is introduced by the character Doc Daneeka, an army psychiatrist who invokes 'Catch-22' to explain why any pilot requesting mental evaluation for insanity, hoping to be found not sane enough to fly and thereby escape dangerous missions, demonstrates his own sanity in creating the request and thus cannot be declared insane. Here is the first time it is mentioned in the novel: "You mean there's a catch?"

"Sure there's a catch," Doc Daneeka replied. "Catch-22. Anyone who wants to get out of combat duty isn't really crazy."

"Pop Goes the Weasel"

Meaning: a surprise or sudden action.

Origin: One popular theory is based on Cockney rhyming slang, where 'popping' is slang for pawning and that weasel may be a corruption of 'whistle and flute', rhyming slang for suit or 'weasel and stoat, rhyming slang for coat. In other words, 'popping the weasel' was slang for needing to sell one's clothes to pay debt. The only issue with this theory is that these rhyming slang words appear in the 1930s and the popular nursery rhyme appears 80 years earlier.

The earliest known published version is the title of a dance tune 'Pop goes the weasel' and the accompanying dance became something of a craze in the 1850s, so much so that in early 1853 the fashionable location of Bath considered worthwhile to place an advertisement in the Bath Chronicle, offering instruction for the highly fashionable dance of 'Pop Goes the Weasel'.

The dance didn't have lyrics as such. It was a jig and 'pop goes the weasel' was shouted out at significant points to accentuate the dance.

Shortly after this, the nursery rhyme appears and there are different variations across both America and the United Kingdom although both have the 'pop' and 'weasel' words in with the same melody. The song was the popular choice for the 'jack in the box' toy which became regularly available in 1935 as it was mass manufactured, although it was an expensive gift for the rich centuries before this and the popular nursery rhyme.

"Egged On"

Meaning: to urge or encourage someone to do something that is usually foolish or dangerous.

Origin: The verb 'eggede', from which the phrase to egg someone on is derived, has been in the English language since approximately 1200. 'Eggede' at this point is a variation of 'edge' or 'urge', so to 'eggede' was simply to 'urge' or 'edge' someone on to do something. It is derived from the Old Norse word 'eddja', which means to incite or provoke and has nothing to do with chickens whatsoever.

The idiom 'to egg someone on' first appeared in Thomas Drant's translation of Horace (*Quintus Horatius Flaccus*), the Roman poet (65–8BC) '*Horace his arte of poetrie, pistles and satyrs englished*', 1566: "*Ile egge them on to speake some thyng, whiche spoken may repent them.*"

"Cut the Mustard"

Meaning: to be sufficient for something or of high enough quality.

Origin: There is no definitive origin for this phrase. The most common theory however is based on mustard being one of the main crops hundreds of years ago, it was cut by hand with scythes, in the same way as corn. The crop could grow up to six feet high and this was notoriously hard work, requiring extremely sharp tools. When blunt they would not 'cut the mustard'.

The phrase in its current guise emerged in the USA towards the end of the nineteenth century. The earliest example found in print is from the Kansas newspaper '*The Ottawa Herald*', 1889: "He tried to run the post office business under Cleveland's administration, but couldn't cut the mustard."

"Like a Bull in a China Shop"

Meaning: behaving recklessly and clumsily in a situation where one is likely to cause damage.

Origin: The phrase comes from literally imagining a bull in a shop that sells crockery, also known as china, from its close association with the Chinese pottery markets.

The first example in print is found in America in Frederick Marryat's book, 'Jacob Faithful', 1834: "Whatever it is that smashes, Mrs T. always swears it was the most valuable thing in the room. I'm like a bull in a china shop."

The phrase must be older than the book as clearly it is recognised in a novel, however it won't be much older, as fine porcelain, known as 'China', was not introduced to Europe and the Americas until the 1600s and not manufactured there until the 1800s, when presumably the phrase came to life as it was very valuable at the time.

"Like a Bat Out of Hell"

Meaning: to move extremely fast or aggressively.

Origin: You may be surprised to hear that the saying predates Meatloaf's popular album of 1977, although he is certainly responsible for the popularity of the saying now.

In fact, the term is used in an ancient play 'The Birds' by Aristophanes, first performed in 414 BC. "He offered a little victim, a camel, slit his throat and, following the example of Ulysses, stepped one pace backwards. Then that bat of a Chaerephon came up from hell to drink the camel's blood."

The first recorded version used in the exact way it is today is in Washington DC paper, 'The Evening Star', 1895: "Toiling up the terrible grade, one horse on the cook's wagon gave out, and four of the cowboys hitched their lariats to the pole and jerked the wagon up the gulch like a bat out o' hell."

Many ancient books depict bats as dark creatures that are associated with hell or the devil and it is believed this is where the association comes from.

"Cock and Bull Story"

Meaning: an implausible story used as an explanation or excuse.

Origin: One famous theory for the origin of 'cock and bull' lies with the Cock and the Bull coaching inns in the town of Stony Stratford in Buckinghamshire, UK. It is said the banter and rivalry between groups of travellers there at the height of the coaching era, eighteenth and early nineteenth centuries, is said to have resulted in exaggerated and fanciful stories, which became known as 'cock and bull stories'. The two hostelries did, and still do, exist but there is no evidence that this is the actual origin.

Experts now believe the origin lies with the seventeenth century French term *'coq-a-l'âne'* which was covered in Randle Cotgrave's 'A Dictionarie of the French and English Tongues', 1611, as meaning: "An incoherent story, passing from one subject to another." This term must have already been understood for it to be in a dictionary.

The literal translation of *'du coq à l'âne'* is 'from rooster to jackass', which nicely fits the meaning of the term. This was later taken up in gaelic as 'cockalayne', again with the same meaning.

The first direct citation of 'cock and bull' in English is from the English dramatist John Day, in the comic play 'Law-trickes', 1608: "That boy is worth his weight in pearle, do pay attention to what a tale of a Cock and a Bull he told my father while I made thee and the rest away." The age of this story further disproves the coaching inn theory as it predates the coaching era.

"Bigger Bang for Your Buck"

Meaning: better value for one's money or exertion.

Origin: The phrase originated from the American slang usage of the words 'bang', which means 'excitement' and 'buck' which means a dollar or money in general.

The first printed example of the phrase in print is an advert in 'Metals and Plastics Publications', 1940, presumably the phrase is already understood at this point though as no company would advertise a saying that is not readily understood.

The phrase 'bigger bang for the buck' was famously used by U.S. President Dwight D. Eisenhower's Secretary of Defense, Charles Erwin Wilson in 1954 when describing the need for larger nuclear weapons and the phrase can be seen used far more regularly from this point.

"Moving the Goal Posts"

Meaning: unfairly alter the conditions or rules of a procedure during its course.

Origin: This phrase is a straightforward derivation from sports that use goalposts and that moving them would clearly be a disadvantage to one of the teams.

The earliest sporting example found in print is from Scottish newspaper 'The Forfar Dispatch', 1946: "Shift the goalposts, said someone as the seasiders repeatedly finished wide of the mark."

The figurative use alludes to the perceived unfairness in changing any goal one may be trying to achieve after the process one is engaged in has already started. The figurative use is a relatively new one and seems to come to the fore in the 1980s.

The earliest figurative example found in print is from the Jamaican newspaper 'The Gleaner', quoting British Chancellor of the Exchequer, Nigel Lawson, 1987: "I see no reason to move the goalposts at all."

"Away With the Fairies"

Meaning: giving the impression of being mad, distracted, or in a dreamworld.

Origin: This phrase originated from Scottish or Irish/Gaelic myths. It was referenced in print in a letter written by William Drummond, a Scottish bard, in 1636: "As for the Fairy Queen, of whom you wrote to me, her Apparitions of late have bewitched so many, that I find sundry ready to dance with the fairies." Although this is not the exact phrase 'away with the fairies', the meaning behind this is of fairies taking away people or bewitching them.

The exact phrase 'away with the fairies' was first mentioned in a New Zealand newspaper, the 'Otautau Standard and Wallace County Chronicle', 1909. The paper retold an Irish character, Michael Coyne, in a story where he was trying to convince the audience that his rival has gone 'away with fairies' and had not been killed by him. Since then, the phrase has become popular in many writings.

"Cats Have 9 Lives"

Meaning: cats and their notorious longevity and guile in dangerous situations.

Origin: There is no definitive origin behind this one but the most popular notion behind why cats have 'nine lives' specifically came from the ancient Egyptian reverence of cats. The god Atum-Ra took the form of a cat when visiting the underworld and gave birth to eight other major gods. Therefore, Atum unified nine lives in one.

The myth that cats have multiple lives exists in many cultures around the world however, it is not always nine lives, and the number varies from different cultures. Some Spanish-speaking regions believe cats have seven lives, while Turkish and Arabic legends claim cats have six lives.

Although we cannot give a definitive origin the saying has been around for centuries, even William Shakespeare using it in 1596 in Romeo and Juliet: Tybalt. "What wouldst thou have with me? Mercutio: good king of cats, nothing but one of your nine lives."

"Mad as a Hatter"

Meaning: insane or crazy.

Origin: The use of mercury in hat making in the 1800s and the resulting effects causing shaking when over exposed are well known. Mercury poisoning is still known today as 'Mad Hatter's disease'. The evidence of this as the origin of the saying is only circumstantial though and beyond the fact that hat makers often suffered trembling fits due to poisoning and although there's no evidence that this is the origin of 'as mad as a hatter' it is thought the most likely reason.

The earliest printed example of the phrase is from Blackwood's 'Edinburgh Magazine', 1829: "He's raving, demented, mad as a hatter." The phrase can be seen numerous times in print after this so was clearly in use by this time.

Shortly after this, in 1865, we see Lewis Carrol's character 'Hatter' in his book 'Alice's adventures in wonderland' and although he is never named as 'mad', we do see the Cheshire Cat character say: "'In that direction, the Cat said, lives a hatter, and in That direction, lives a March Hare. Visit either you like, they're both mad." It is thought that the story popularised the saying 'Mad as a Hatter' to a much larger audience.

"Give Free Rein"

Meaning: give someone freedom to do what they want.

Origin: The expression 'free rein' originated from horseback riding and refers to the act of holding the reins that control the horse loosely so as to allow the horse to freely move along at its own pace and in its desired direction. The saying originally had the correct spelling for 'reins', as in the straps that control a horse, and the saying is quite often quoted more recently as 'reigns', which is incorrect.

The first time it can be found in print is in reference to letting a horse go where it chooses is in Alexander Read's 'The Chirurgicall Lectures of Tumors and Ulcers', 1635: "When we give it free reins to lash out."

Two hundred and fifty years later, we see the phrase being used as 'reign' (incorrectly) and by this point is being used figuratively. This can be found first in print in the American book 'The Salvator and Scientist', 1896: "Here we may give free reign to our imagination, with the moral certainty that science will supply nothing tending either to prove or to disprove any of its fancies."

"Houston, We Have a Problem"

Meaning: used to explain something has gone wrong.

Origin: The famous line was first used by astronaut John Swigert Jr on the USA's Apollo 13 moon flight. John Swigert Jr reported a problem back to their base in Houston on 14th April, 1970, although the original quote is slightly different to that seen in the film. 'Okay, Houston, we've had a problem here' is what was actually said.

Swigert used the phrase to report a major technical fault in the electrical system of one of the Service Module's oxygen tanks.

'Houston, we have a problem' was used later as the tagline for the 1995 film – Apollo 13. It is the dialogue of the film, edited for dramatic effect, that is now best remembered.

The phrase has since come to be used in a multitude of scenarios where there is a problem.

"First Dibs"

Meaning: said to establish a claim on something.

Origin: The origin of 'Dibs' is thought to originate in a game played by children called dib-stones which used pebbles or the knucklebones of sheep. The game was known since the late seventeenth century in the UK. The game, which involved the claiming of the 'dib-stones' by calling out 'dibs' is how 'first dibs' is thought to have originated.

'Dib-stones' is known to have been played since 1693 as it was recorded in the English philosopher Jock Locke's 'Some Thoughts Concerning Education', which was published that year: "I have seen little Girls exercise whole Hours together and take abundance of Pains to be expert at Dibstones as they call it."

'Dibs' or 'Dib-stones', originated in England but all of the early citations of 'first dibs' specifically are from the USA. It is entirely plausible that the 'claim' meaning of 'dibs' travelled to the USA from England as people migrated there. Any child who called out 'dibs' when playing 'dib-stones' would surely continue to do so whether in Olde England or New England.

'First dibs' was certainly in use in the USA by the early 1900s and can be seen first when the Wisconsin Home and Farm School Association published a pamphlet called 'Our Boys', 1907: "I got first dibs on the baking pan."

"Ship Shape"

Meaning: in good order, trim and neat.

Origin: The term 'ship shape' is of nautical origin and is based on the obligation of a sailor to keep his or her quarters arranged neatly and securely due to the limited space typically allotted to service members aboard ship, and against turbulence at sea. The original term was 'ship shapen', 'shapen' meant wrought with a definite shape.

The first recorded version of it can be seen in Sir Henry Manwayring's 'The sea-man's dictionary', 1644: "It being of no use for the Ship, but only for to make her Ship shapen, as they call it."

The word has since become a figurative meaning for anything that is tidy or in good order.

"Wind of Change"

Meaning: a shift in power or policy.

Origin: The 'Wind of Change' speech was a famous address made by British Prime Minister Harold Macmillan to the Parliament of South Africa in Cape Town in 1960. He had spent a month in Africa in visiting a number of British colonies and the following statement was used: "The wind of change is blowing through this continent. Whether we like it or not, this growth of national consciousness is a political fact."

The phrase came to be used wherever there was a change in the air politically or otherwise and was popularised soon after by the Rock group 'The Scorpions' in 1990 with their song 'wind of change'.

"Put On Your Thinking Cap"

Meaning: take time for consideration of something.

Origin: A 'thinking cap' was previously known by the name a 'considering cap'. That term has gone entirely out of use now but was known since at least the early seventeenth century, as in this example from Robert Armin in 'Foole upon foole', 1605: "The Cobler puts off his considering cap, why sir, sayes he, I sent them home but now."

The earliest record for the term 'thinking cap' is from the USA, in the Wisconsin newspaper The Kenosha Times, July 1857: "This tendency is a very good thing as the safeguard of our independence from the control of foreign power, and it obliges every man to keep his thinking cap on."

There is no physical evidence of a 'considering cap' or 'thinking cap' being an actual piece of clothing throughout history and therefore the thought is that both were only ever used as figurative terms. Many believe that the fictional character Sherlock Holmes may be the reason behind the term, unfortunately the term predates the stories.

"At Sixes and Sevens"

Meaning: in a state of total confusion or disarray.

Origin: The phrase was originally 'to set on six and seven' and is thought to have derived in the fourteenth century from the game of dice. The meaning then was 'to carelessly risk one's entire fortune'. The earliest citation in print is Chaucer's 'Troilus and Criseyde', 1374: *"Lat nat this wrechched wo thyn herte gnawe.* But manly set the world on sexe and seuene."

The first appearance of the term as it is now, 'at sixes and sevens', was in 1670, in 'Leti's Il cardinalismo di Santa Chiesa', translated by G. H, 1670: "They leave things at sixes and sevens."

Over time, the phrase has come to mean anything or anyone in a state of disarray or utter confusion, not just in trouble in a game.

"Putting One's Foot in One's Mouth"

Meaning: to say something foolish, embarrassing or tactless.

Origin: This term is thought to have come from the earlier phrase, 'to put one's foot in it', which is in reference to standing in something one would not want to. This term is first found in print in 'Polite conversation' by author Jonathan Swift, 1738: "The bishop has put his foot in it."

The exact term 'Putting one's foot in one's mouth' is found first in print in a book of slang in 1823 so must already be understood at this point. Some believe it is in reference to 'foot and mouth disease' which is found in cows but there is no written evidence of this.

A clearer definition can be found in P W Joyce's 'English as we speak', 1910: "To a person who habitually uses unfortunate blundering expressions, you never open your mouth, but you put your foot in it."

"Left in the Lurch"

Meaning: to be left abandoned or without assistance.

Origin: This phrase originates from the French board game of '*lourche*' or lurch, which was similar to backgammon and has not been played since the 1600s.

The game came to England from continental Europe and its name is thought to derive from the German word for 'left', which is '*lurtsch*'. Players with no points would be stuck on the left side of the board.

Players suffered a lurch if they were left in a hopeless position from which they couldn't win the game, very similar to check mate in chess. The card game of cribbage, or crib, also has a 'lurch' position which players may be left in if they don't progress halfway round the peg board before the winner finishes.

The figurative usage of the phrase can first be seen in print in 'Nashe's Saffron Walden', 1596: "Whom he also procured to be equally bound with him for his new cousens apparence to the law, which he neuer did, but left both of them in the lurtch for him."

"On a Wing and a Prayer"

Meaning: with only the slightest chance of success.

Origin: This saying originated in World War 2. The earliest reference found is in the 1942 film 'The Flying Tigers'. In the film, John Wayne's character, Captain Jim Gordon, says this in a reference to the flight of replacement pilots: Gordon: "Any word on that flight yet?"

Rangoon hotel clerk: "Yes, sir, it was attacked and fired on by Japanese aircraft. She's coming in on one wing and a prayer."

The phrase was taken up by songwriters Harold Adamson and Jimmie McHugh in their patriotic song, 'Coming in on a Wing and a Prayer', 1943, which tells of a damaged warplane, barely able to limp back to base:

♫Comin' in on a wing and a prayer, Comin' in on a wing and a prayer, though there's one motor gone, We can still carry on, Comin' in on a wing and a prayer♫

The phrase then became popular with the public and there are many references to it in US newspapers from 1943 onwards. It was taken up by Hollywood and a film, 'Wing and a Prayer', was released in 1944.

"In Fine Fettle"

Meaning: in good condition, healthy or feeling good.

Origin: 'Fettle' is what is known as a fossil word, which means a word that is no longer used. It is only really seen in the modern language in this particular idiom. Fettle means status or condition and is thought to derive from the Middle English word 'fetlen', which means to prepare or put into shape.

The word 'fettle' is first seen in print in Anne Bronte's 'Agnes Grey', 1847: "But next day, afore I'd gotten fettled up, for indeed, Miss, I'd no heart to sweeping an' fettling an' washing pots, so I sat me down i' th' muck." The word is thought to be much older though and is presumably readily understood for it to appear in a novel.

The first time we see the full term in print is in Jack London's 'John Barleycorn', 1913: "Those fifty-one days of fine sailing and intense sobriety had put me in splendid fettle."

"Pull the Wool Over One's Eyes"

Meaning: to trick or deceive someone.

Meaning: Although there is no definitive evidence, the common theory is that this phrase derives from the wearing of woollen wigs, which were fashionable for both men and women in the sixteenth and seventeenth centuries. The theory is a literal one in that a wig fallen from one's head would block what can be seen.

The phrase itself is of nineteenth century American origin. The earliest example of it in print is found in the Gettysburg newspaper 'The People's Press', 1835: "We are glad to find among the leading Van-ites, at least one man, whose conscience will not permit him to 'go the whole hog' in 'pulling the wool over the people's eyes'."

"Flip One's Lid"

Meaning: suddenly lose control or become very angry.

Origin: Experts believe this phrase is an allusion to a kettle boiling over and is used figuratively to an individual 'losing one's cool'. Other examples of a kettle being used figuratively to explain someone being out of control or angry are 'steam coming out of one's ears', 'boiling over' and 'blowing one's top'.

There is no physical evidence of this, but it is certainly logical. What we can say is the phrase has been around for at least 70 years with the first example found in print in 'The New York Times' in a book review, 1951: "The funniest book of the lot is enough to make a reader 'flip' or 'flip his lid'."

"Guts for Garters"

Meaning: a threat of punishment, usually said in jest to another.

Origin: The threat 'to have someone's guts for garters' was never meant to be taken literally, even in Tudor England, where the expression originated. At that time, disembowelment was used as a form of torture and execution. The punishment of 'hanged, drawn and quartered' was on the statue book in England until as late as 1790 and this is why and where the saying came from.

Although the threat wasn't a real one, it at least would have made sense then as garters were then worn by men as a way of holding up their stockings. Garters aren't commonly worn now, and the expression has followed them into relative obscurity.

These days, the expression is limited to figurative examples, like, "I don't want to tell Dad that I've scraped the car, he'll have my guts for garters."

The first printed reference to 'guts for garters' appears in Robert Greene's 'The Scottish Historie of James the Fourth', 1592: "Ile make garters of thy guttes, Thou villaine."

"Smoke and Mirrors"

Meaning: the obscuring or embellishing of the truth.

Origin: 'Smoke and mirrors' is a classic illusionist's technique that makes something appear to float in empty space. It was first documented in 1770 and spread widely after its use by the illusionist Johann Georg Schröpfer, who claimed the apparitions to be conjured spirits.

It subsequently became a fixture of nineteenth-century phantasmagoria shows. The illusion relies on a hidden projector, known then as a magic lantern, the beam of which reflects off a mirror into a cloud of smoke, which in turn scatters the beam to create an image.

The first figurative use is seen much later and can be seen in print when American journalist Jimmy Breslin' notes from Impeachment, 1975: "All political power is primarily an illusion, mirrors and blue smoke."

The phrase 'smoke and mirrors' has entered into common English use to refer to any proposal that, when examined closely, proves to be an illusion.

"Pass the Buck"

Meaning: shift the responsibility for something to someone else.

Origin: Contrary to what you many think, the 'buck' in question here is nothing to do with the American Dollar. Poker players were highly suspicious of cheating or any form of bias and there's considerable folklore depicting gunslingers in shoot-outs based on accusations of dirty dealing.

In order to avoid unfairness, the deal changed hands during sessions. The person who was next in line to deal would be given a marker. This was usually a knife, and knives often had handles made of buck's horn – hence the marker becoming known as a buck. When the dealer's turn was done, he 'passed the buck'.

The earliest citation of the phrase found in print is from the Weekly New Mexican, July 1865: "They draw at the commissary, and at poker after they have passed the 'buck'".

The figurative version of the phrase, that is, a usage where no actual buck is present is first seen in print in the California newspaper 'The Oakland Tribune', 1902: "When the public or the Council 'pass the buck' up to me I am going to act."

"Top Drawer"

Meaning: of the finest quality or class.

Origin: This phrase comes from the Victorian gentry, who kept their most valuable items, such as jewellery, in the highest drawer of a bedroom chest of drawers. This was where the phrase 'top-drawer' came from and was initially used to denote a person's level of social standing, based on their family background. Families were either 'top-drawer' or they weren't.

The earliest example found in print comes shortly after the Victorian era (1837–1901) in the novel 'The hill, a romance of friendship' by English writer Horace Vachell, 1905: "You'll find plenty of fellows abusing Harrow, he said quietly, but take it from me, that the fault lies not in Harrow, but in them. Such boys, as a rule, do not come out of the top drawer."

"Left Holding the Bag/Baby"

Meaning: to be made responsible for a problem that nobody else wants to deal with.

Origin: To be 'left holding the bag' is more of an American term, the most common British term meaning the same thing is 'left holding the baby'. Both effectively mean the same thing – to be left with the responsibility or blame of all.

The original American term was to 'give somebody the bag to hold' and experts believe the logical explanation of where the term comes from lies with the act of bank robbery and just one individual caught with the 'swag'. The term can be seen used figuratively as early as 1793 in the writings of Thomas Jefferson: "She will leave Spain to hold the bag."

The British version, meaning the same thing comes later and is first seen in print in 'The Glasgow Herald', 1875: "The shrewder of the operators are getting out quietly, but, in Stock Exchange phrase, some will be left to 'hold the baby'."

"The Bucket List"

Meaning: a number of experiences or achievements that a person hopes to accomplish during their lifetime.

Origin: Bucket list's origins aren't as old as you might assume. The 2007 film *'The Bucket List'* introduced many people to this common phrase and it isn't found in print before this.

Although no one knows for certain if the phrase existed earlier, screenwriter Justin Zackham got the idea for the movie after creating his own 'bucket list'. Zackham originally called his list 'Justin's list of things to do before he kicks the bucket'.

Kick the bucket is a much older phrase I have covered before and is first found in print in the 'Dictionary of the Vulgar Tongue', 1785.

"Two Cents Worth"

Meaning: said when an individual offers you their ideas and views or opinion.

Origin: Although there is no definitive origin of this phrase, the common theory is that 'two cents worth' was the minimum wage required of a new player in order to enter poker games.

The US version of the phrase is pre-dated by the British 'two-penneth worth' and there's little reason to believe 'two cents' worth' to be anything other than a US translation of that. The card-playing origin of the phrase could just as well apply to the British version but, without evidence, that's merely speculation.

The earliest example found in print of the US-variant is from the 'Orlean Evening Times', 1926. That includes an item by Allene Sumner, headed My 'Two cents' worth'.

Etymologists believe the most likely explanation of the British version is related to a much older sixteenth century expression, 'a penny for your thoughts'. So by offering your two penn'orth, meaning two pennies worth, you were perhaps offering a very strong opinion on an issue, although there is no conclusive evidence of this either.

The first time we see two penn'orth in print is in relation to the cost of postage in Britain in 1805 where we see the tuppenny post for the first time. This was the cost of postage at the time.

"Keep One's Ear to the Ground"

Meaning: to be observant and to pay attention to what is going on around you.

Origin: The most common theory behind this idiom refers to the Native-American practice of putting one's ear to the ground in order to detect the vibration of sounds, such as horse hooves approaching in the distance before they can actually be heard.

The first mention in print of the phrase in relation to this is by French author and diplomat François-René de Chateaubriand in 'Voyage en Amérique' (Travel in America), 1827: (Translated into English in 1828) "The foot-prints having been minutely examined, the Indians clap their ears to the ground, and judge, by murmurs inaudible to a European ear, at what distance the enemy is."

The practice of putting one's ear to the ground is not solely of Native Americans however as there is an earlier example found in print of the practice in relation to sailing. The earliest example of this is in 'The Northampton Mercury', 1773: "Notice is given when a Ship arrives, by firing a Gun at the rising of the Sun, and two at its setting, which the Pilots, by laying their Ears to the Ground, declare they can hear at a very great Distance."

The practice in both examples will predate what is found in print but I will leave it to you decide which came first.

"Take It as Read"

Meaning: to accept something as true.

Origin: This phrase is often mis-spelt with the colour red rather than the meaning of something that has already been read in a book or document which is the correct spelling.

Although not conclusive, the phrase is thought to have originated in political or legal speak as this is where all the earliest versions originate. It is common, for instance, for members of a group to accept the minutes of previous meetings 'as read', meaning without objection, or to approve a resolution as presented to the group without modification or the debate that would ensue.

The Oxford English dictionary dates the oldest version found in print as 1811: "Petitions, all of which were taken as read, and ordered to lie on the table." Presumably, the phrase is older than this though as it is clearly understood at the point of the quote.

"Not What It's Cracked Up to Be"

Meaning: disappointing or not as good as expected.

Origin: The 'crack' in this phrase derives in the United Kingdom, where the earliest use of 'crack' can be seen used in terminology other than something that is broken or fractured.

A book on the speech of Northern England published in 1825 states 'crack' means to chat, have conversation or share news. Reading between the lines if something is not what 'it's cracked up to be' it would mean not as good as was talked about.

The term is recorded in Scotland in this sense as far back as the sixteenth century, with both Robert Fergusson and Robert Burns using it in the 1770s and 1780s. There are other expressions using 'crack' in this manner found in the 1900s such as 'What's the crack'.

'Crack', may have its origins in the UK, but the full expression is not found in print until the year 1835 in a quote by American folk hero, Davy Crockett, who was a politician at the time. He is quoted as having said the phrase when commenting on someone running for president: "Martin Van Buren is not the man he is cracked up to be."

#history #origins #facts #linkedin

"Spend a Penny"

Meaning: a need to urinate.

Origin: This saying comes from the earliest public toilets, which had locks on the doors which cost a penny to open. This practice appears to have begun in the 1850s, when the first public toilets were opened in London, however the phrase wasn't recorded in literature until nearly a century later.

The first recorded citation of it is in H. Lewis's 'Strange Story', 1945: "Us girls," she said, "are going to spend a penny."

"Simple Simon"

Meaning: a foolish or gullible person.

Origin: The verses used in the nursery rhyme today are the first of a longer chapbook history first published in 1764. The Simon in question here is thought to be Simon Edy, known as Old Simon, who was a London beggar who lived in a derelict 'Rats' Castle' in the rookery of Dyott Street. He was born in Woodford in Northamptonshire in 1709 and died on 18 May 1783.

He begged outside the churchyard of St Giles in the Fields and was a well-known figure, being portrayed by artists including John Seago and Thomas Rowlandson. As he was known as a 'simpleton', he is thought to be a possible inspiration for the nursery rhyme, 'Simple Simon', which was published in the Royal Book of Nursery Rhymes nearby in Monmouth Court.

"My Hands Are Tied"

Meaning: unable to act freely because something prevents you from doing so.

Origin: This phrase alludes figuratively to having one's hands physically restrained because they were bound by someone else. Restraining one's hands has historically been the way of restraining someone for many generations, so it is easy to understand how this figurative phrase came to be.

This phrase in its current figurative meaning is first seen in print in clergyman Thomas Fuller's 'The Holy state and the Profane State', 1642: "When God intends a nation shall be beaten, he ties their hands behind them."

Clearly hands being tied physically can be seen in print many times before this, but the figurative meaning seems to be understood in the early 1600s.

"High and Dry"

Meaning: without resources or help.

Origin: This term originally referred to ships that were beached. The 'dry' implies that, not only were they out of the water, but had been for some time and could be expected to remain so.

The first record found in print is in a 'Ship News' column in 'The London Times', 1796: "The Russian frigate Archipelago, yesterday got aground below the Nore at high water, which; when the tide had ebbed, left her nearly high and dry."

The term has since come to be used figuratively for anything or anyone left struggling without help.

"Showing Someone the Ropes"

Meaning: show someone how to do a particular job or task.

Origin: The origin of this expression is not from boxing as is commonly thought but from sailing ships, where the sailors had to get to know the complicated system of ropes which made up the rigging. To sailors every part of the standing rigging and running rigging had a name, and in these name's the word 'rope' was rarely used.

There were halliards, braces, sheets, lifts, clew-lines, buntlines and many more, as if sailors deliberately avoided the word 'rope'. This is possibly because the 'rope' in times gone by meant 'the hangman's hempen haul' or a flogging with a 'rope's end'.

Although this expression is thought to be centuries old, the first time it can be found in print is as late as 1940 in 'Two years before the mast' by Richard H. Dana: "The captain, who had been on the coast before and 'knew the ropes', took the steering oar, and we went off in the same way as the other boat."

"Flogging a Dead Horse"

Meaning: to waste effort on something when there is no chance of succeeding.

Origin: The origin of the expression 'flogging a dead horse' comes from the mid-nineteenth century, when the practice of beating horses to make them go faster was often viewed as acceptable. To flog a dead horse would be pointless, as clearly it wouldn't be able to go anywhere.

The earliest example found in print is in London newspaper, the 'Watchman and Wesleyan Advertiser', 1859: "It was notorious that Mr Bright was dissatisfied with his winter reform campaign and rumour said that he had given up his effort with the exclamation that it was like flogging a dead horse."

"If the Cap Fits"

Meaning: if something applies to you, accept it.

Origin: It is similar in meaning to another saying, 'if the shoe fits, wear it'. This expression originated from the older saying if the cap fits.

The cap in question is that of the fool and dates from the early 1700s. The point being, if you have the cap of a fool, you probably are a fool.

"Grab the Bull by the Horns"

Meaning: to do something difficult in a determined and confident way.

Origin: The exact origin of this phrase is unknown. There are two trains of thought, the first is that it originated in bullfighting around 1800. The term most likely alludes to grasping a safely tethered bull, not one the matador is fighting in the ring.

The other theory is that the idiom's origin is actually from the American West. Instead of bullfighting, it found its roots in rodeos where it was common for ranchers and cowhands to attempt their luck at steer wrestling. It is said that the only way to control and bring down a steer (young bull) was to grab it by the horns. If a person tried to grab anywhere else, they stood the risk of getting bashed by the horns.

Though the location of origin is not certain, what is certain is that the saying has been around since the 1800s and that it's probably not a good idea to actually do it!

"Tickled Pink"

Meaning: very happy or amused.

Origin: This saying alludes to one's face turning pink with laughter when one is being tickled. The first example found in print is in 1910, in an Illinois' newspaper – 'The Daily Review', in a piece titled 'Lauder Tickled at Change': "Grover Laudermilk was tickled pink over Kinsella's move in buying him from St Louis."

The saying must be older than this however as the newspaper is published in a way that would make you believe the audience would understand the story. There are other examples of being tickled silly as early as 1800 but the 'pink' variation must be around the turn of the twentieth century as it cannot be found earlier in print than the above newspaper.

"Going the Extra Mile"

Meaning: to do more than one is required.

Origin: This phrase is an adaptation of a commandment of Jesus in 'the Sermon of Mount' (Matthew Ch 5 v 41): "And whosoever shall compel thee to go a mile, go with him twain."

Under the Roman Impressment Law, a Roman soldier passing by a Jew could order him to carry his pack for one mile. Jesus asked his followers to go two miles instead of one.

"Yellow Bellied"

Meaning: a cowardly person.

Origin: It is not clear what literal connection there is between yellow bellies and cowards. One thought is that yellow belly refers to the way some animals roll over and play dead when they give up.

The first it is seen in print is in England as a nickname for people from the Lincolnshire Fens. This area of England is marshy and contains eels. The term is found in Francis Grose's 1787 'A provincial glossary; with a collection of local proverbs etc': "Yellow bellies. This is an appellation given to persons born in the Fens, who, it is jocularly said, have yellow bellies, like their eels."

This original use may not be connected to the American usage which first appeared in print in the United States in 1842 in 'The Wisconsin Enquirer': "It is the intention of the Texans to 'keep dark' until the Mexicans cross Colorado, and then give them a San Jacinto fight, with an army from 5000 to 7000 men. God send that they may bayonet every 'yellow belly' in the Mexican army."

"Right up My Alley/Street"

Meaning: the kind of thing you like or know about.

Origin: the expression 'right up your street' is the British English version of the expression whilst in American English the phrase, with the same meaning, is 'right up your alley'. In both the British and American versions, the word 'up' is interchangeable with 'down' and is used just as often.

There is no definite origin of the expression although the first recorded usage of the metaphorical usage of the American expression dates to 1931. It can be found in M.E. Gilman's Sob Sister v.65 and reads "It's about time a good murder broke, and this one is right up your alley."

The first usage of the British English expression can be traced back earlier than its American equivalent to the year 1929. This can be found in the 'Publishers' Weekly' magazine and reads "A great many of the books published today are, as the saying is, right up her street."

"Raw Deal"

Meaning: an instance of unfair treatment.

Origin: The 'Raw' in this expression, which originated in America, means 'Crude'. The first it is found in print is in a 1912 Canadian dictionary where the term is defined as 'A swindle', a meaning also rarely heard today. The 'Raw' here means unfinished, uncooked or not ready, so not very good or fair.

"Burning the Candle at Both Ends"

Meaning: to work or do other things from early in the morning until late at night and so get very little rest.

Origin: The term *burn the candle at both ends* is derived from the French phrase '*Brusler la chandelle par les deux bouts*'. Coined around the beginning of the seventeenth century, the early meaning of *burn the candle at both ends* was to be a spendthrift, to be wasteful.

Candles were expensive and burning both ends of a candle used it up much faster. Eventually, the candle in question came to symbolise one's life force and *burning the candle at both ends* meant to use of one's life force too quickly, to exhaust oneself by working too much.

"A Little Bird Told Me"

Meaning: used to say that you have heard a piece of information about someone from someone else.

Origin: The popular theory for this idiom is that it originates in 'Ecclesiastes', one of the Ketuvim of the Hebrew Bible which was written 450–200 BC the following translation can be found: "Do not revile the king even in your thoughts, or curse the rich in your bedroom, because a bird in the sky may carry your words, and a bird on the wing may report what you say."

Another explanation however is a simple allusion to carrier pigeons or other such messenger birds. John Heywood's 'Proverbs', gives another similar expression, 1562: "I hear by one bird that in mine ear was late chanting, and characterises 'a little bird told me' as the 'modern' version."

We can't be sure on this one but certainly we can say that birds have been giving us messages for more than two millennia and it is likely the current saying has evolved from these earlier examples.

"Top Gun"

Meaning: one who is at the **top** in ability, rank or prestige.

Origin: The Navy Fighter Weapons School, the official name for Topgun, was created in response to the poor performance of U.S. Navy fighters and their missiles in the first few years of the air war over North Vietnam.

Things were rated in Kill ratio, that is the number of enemy's killed by missiles/fighters/air combat compared to 'home' soldiers lost. As for Vietnam aerial combat, Topgun training and other measures resulted in a reported increase in the Navy's kill ratio to 13-to-1 by the end of the war from 2.5-to-1 at the beginning.

"A Horse of a Different Colour"

Meaning: an unrelated or only incidentally related matter with distinctly different significance.

Origin: The origin for this term is thought to derive from a slightly different phrase first coined by Shakespeare, who wrote in his story 'Twelfth Night', 1601–02: 'A horse of that colour', meaning 'the same matter' rather than a different one.

By the mid-1800s, as with many idioms or phrases we start to see the term adapted and used to point out difference rather than likeness.

"Go Apesh*t"

Meaning: to become crazy, enraged, excited or out of control.

Origin: A common suggestion for the origin of go ape is that it came from the 1933 movie King Kong although there is no evidence to support this 'sh*t' is often used as a slang intensifier: bullsh*t, chickensh*t, batsh*t. The enduring popularity of bullsh*t (which in the sense of 'falsehood'/'nonsense' is actually of much more recent vintage than the equivalent 'bull', despite what one may assume) probably inspired the others.

Apesh*t can therefore be traced to ape (in the 'going ape' sense), just as batsh*t can be traced to batty or bats. All four basically mean the same thing.

The Oxford English Dictionary lists it as a variant of 'to go ape', with the earliest citation of both being a single entry in a 1955 edition of 'American speech', where they are both listed as 'air force slang'.

"Off Their Rockers" and "Off Their Trolley"

Meaning: Said when a person is behaving in a very strange or silly way.

Origin: This expression originated near the end of the 1800s. 'Off' is a common beginning to expressions signalling mental problems. In some cases, one might simply say, "Something about him seems off."

Other similar examples are 'off one's head', 'off the rails' and 'off one's trolley'.

It is though that all these examples come from the same thing, 'Off one's trolley' came first, appearing in print in 1896 and 'Off one's rocker' appeared just a year later.

The most commonly though idea is related to electrical trams. Some trolleys on the trams need to maintain contact with an overhead wire to receive power. 'Off one's trolley' means that the trolley lost contact with the wire, and lost power. This could make sense for a person's whose brain is no longer receiving a good signal. 'Off one's rocker' could merely be a synonym for 'off one's trolley' although another theory is that the 'rocker' in 'Off one's rocker is a rocking chair which an old person may have fell off. 'Rocker' is first recorded in print as a rocking chair in 1892.

There is no definitive answer for this one, but this is what etymologists believe to be the most likely origin based on the times the phrase is first seen and the invention of the tram system in or around the same time period.

"The Perfect Storm"

Meaning: an especially bad situation caused by a combination of unfavourable circumstances.

Origin: The Oxford English Dictionary has published references going back to 1718 for a 'perfect storm'.

The first use of the expression in the meteorological sense comes from 1850, when the Rev. Lloyd of Withington (Manchester, England) describes "A perfect storm of thunder and lightning all over England doing fearful and fatal damage."

In 1993, journalist and author Sebastian Junger planned to write a book about the 1991 Halloween Nor'easter storm. Junger published his book 'The Perfect Storm' in 1997 and its success brought the phrase into popular culture. Its adoption was accelerated with the release of the 2000 feature film adaptation of Junger's book.

The phrase has since come to be used in a 'worst-case scenario' situation in things not necessarily related to meteorological situations. It was used many times during the financial crisis of 2007–2008.

"Thick As Two Short Planks"

Meaning: very stupid.

Origin: 'Thick' has been used to mean slow-witted or stupid since the turn of the seventeenth century. Shakespeare used it to good effect in *Henry IV, Part. 2*, 1600: "Hang him baboon, his wit's as thicke as Tewksbury mustard."

Here 'thick' does double duty. It refers to the obvious lack of wit that a piece of wood would display and also to another meaning of thick, that is, 'short and wide'. Planks of wood are wide and the shorter they are, the greater their apparent thickness. Two short planks are even thicker.

The expression 'as thick as two short planks', which is sometimes given in the variant form 'as thick as two planks', is of UK origin and dates from the 1970s. The earliest example of it found in print is in Gordon Honeycombe's novel '*Adam's Tale*', 1974. There are numerous examples of 'thick as' with other items too, pig sh*t is another example of this.

"To Add Insult to Injury"

Meaning: act in a way that makes a bad situation worse.

Origin: The idiom 'add insult to injury' has ancient origins. It dates all the way back to the time of the Roman writer Phaedrus, who lived around 15 B.C. to A.D. 50. The origin is first found in print in a passage from the translation of 'Aesop's fables' in 'The Bald Man and the Fly'.

In the story, a bald man is bitten on the head by a fly. In trying to swat the fly, he misses and ends up bonking himself on the head very hard. The fly laughs and says, "You wanted to avenge the prick of a tiny little insect with death. What will you do to yourself, who have added insult to injury?"

"Wrap Your Head Around It"

Meaning: to be unable to understand, believe or come to terms with a situation.

Origin: There is no definitive origin for this phrase but the first time we can see it used appears to have been in a Jim Croce song written in the 1970s. Songwriters tend to reflect language use that are already understood so we can assume that this was already in use from at least the '60s on.

While the expression 'wrap one's head around' something seems to have appeared in the 1970s and may be primarily an American phrase, the term 'get one's head around' something is first seen in print in a 'British boys' magazine in the 1920s.

"The Devil Makes Work for Idle Hands"

Meaning: said to show that you believe people who have nothing to do are more likely to get into trouble or commit a crime.

Origin: The source of this proverb is debatable as there are so many alternative forms of expression that convey the same idea. It is certainly Christian texts of one form or another which were the first to put the proverb into print. For example, the fourth century theologian Jerome expressed the idea in his *Letter:* "*Do something, so that the Devil may always find you busy.*"

The first version to appear in English was in 1405: "*Do some good deeds, so that the Devil, which is our enemy, won't find you unoccupied.*"

The same notion is repeated many times in religious texts throughout the Middle Ages, but it isn't until the nineteenth century that we find the proverb in the form that it is now widely used. Here's an example from *The Indicator*, February 1848: "The boys are not permitted to idle away their time in the streets, for the inhabitants firmly believe that 'the devil finds work for idle hands to do.'"

"Throw in the Towel"

Meaning: abandon a struggle or admit defeat.

Origin: This expression derives from boxing. When a boxer is suffering a beating and his corner want to stop the fight, they literally throw in the towel to indicate their conceding of the fight.

The earliest citation found in print is in the American newspaper '*The Fort Wayne Journal-Gazette*', 1913: "Murphy went after him, landing right and left undefended face. The crowd importuned referee Griffin to stop the fight and a towel was thrown from Burns' corner as a token of defeat."

The expression is likely to be older as it will be readily understood at this point and boxing is an ancient sport. The expression has since transformed into an analogy for anybody who quits at something, not just boxing.

"On the Fiddle"

Meaning: to be engaged in cheating or swindling.

Origin: There are multiple versions of the potential origin of this one.

The most common two are firstly a story of Emperor Nero who played his instrument as Rome burned, some believe this is the fiddle based on his corrupt nature. Unfortunately, fiddles did not exist in this era.

The second being a story of nautical origin where the fiddle is the rim of a plate on a ship and that by being 'on the fiddle' you were right up to the rim and having more than your fair share. Again, this cannot be correct as the fiddle on a ship is nothing to do with plates, in fact it is an arrangement of shelves around a ships table stopping them falling off.

There is no mention of fiddle, in the sense of it meaning to act fraudulently until much later. The term 'fiddle' appears to have originated in America. It is recorded in an 1874 edition of John Hotten's 'A Dictionary of Modern Slang, Cant and Vulgar Words': "Fiddle... In America, a swindle or an imposture."

Hotten also included this entry: "Fiddler... A sharper, a cheat; also one who dawdles over little matters, and neglects great ones."

'On the fiddle' was taken up by the British forces in WWII. It was well enough established in popular slang in the UK by 1961 for it to have been used as the title of a Sean Connery film and that is the first example of it in its current form found in print.

"From Pillar to Post"

Meaning: to move from one place to another with no purpose or direction.

Origin: Etymologists believe the pillars and posts in question here are based in the Middle Ages. At this time when a person is being punished, the person is first tied to a post and whipped and then moved to the pillory where they are showcased to the crowd for their amusement. Hence the original and older phrase 'From Post to Pillar'.

The earlier form of the expression, 'from post to pillar', which has the same meaning as the more modern 'from pillar to post' is first seen in print in John Lydgate's fifteenth century dream poem 'The Assembly of Gods': "Whyche doon he hym sent to Contrycion, And fro thensforth to Satysfaccion; Thus fro poost to pylour he was made to daunce."

The saying 'From pillar to post' comes slightly later in the sixteenth century, when it appeared in print in the Latin book 'Vox Populi', meaning voice of the people, 1550. This was reprinted in W. C. Hazlitt's 'Remains of the early popular poetry of England' in 1866: "From piller vnto post The powr man he was tost."

The expression has since come to be used in any situation where someone has been moved from place to place, often pointlessly. The more common version from the twentieth century being 'Dragged from pillar to post'.

"Stick in One's Craw"

Meaning: to be difficult for one to accept, utter or believe.

Origin: The 'craw', also known 'crop', in question here is that of the preliminary stomach of an animal, particularly birds, where food is pre-digested.

Centuries ago, hunters noticed that some birds swallowed bits of stone that were too large to pass through the craw and into the digestive tract. These stones, unlike the sand and pebbles needed by birds to help grind food in the pouch, literally stuck in the craw and couldn't go down any further.

This expression is a more modern version of stick in one's gizzard, gullet or crop which all refer to an animal's digestive system. The oldest of which can be seen in print in Jonathan Swift's 'Polite conversation', 1738: "Don't let that stick in your gizzard."

"Great Minds Think Alike"

Meaning: said when two people have the same opinion or make the same choice.

Origin: Although this phrase is quite literal in its meaning, its origins are at least 400 years old.

The first reference to the theory that intellectuals share similar thoughts is first recorded in print in 1618 in Dabridgcourt Belchier's 'Hans Beer-Pot': 'Good wits doe jumpe'. 'Jumpe' is an old English word that meant 'agree with' or 'completely coincide'.

Laurence Sterne uses the same terminology in 'The Life and Opinions of Tristram Shandy, Gentleman', 1761: "Great wits jump, for the moment Dr Slop cast his eyes upon his bag the very same thought occurred."

The earliest example of the phrase in its current guise is not found in print until 1816 in Carl Theodor Von Unlanski's biography 'The woeful history of the unfortunate Eudoxia': "It may occur that an editor has already printed something on the identical subject – great minds think alike, you know."

"Nip it in the Bud"

Meaning: to stop something immediately so that it does not become worse.

Origin: This phrase comes from botany, the science of plants. 'Nip in the bud' derives from the de-budding of plants, the bud stage is an early stage of the development of a flower. If you cut off the bud, the flower will not develop.

The analogy of stopping other things early by 'nipping them in the bud' can be found over 400 years ago and the earlier form of the phrase was 'nip in the bloom'. This is first found in print in Henry Chettle's romance 'Piers Plainnes Seaven Yeres Prentiship', 1595: "Extinguish these fond loues with minds labour, and nip thy affections in the bloome, that they may neuer bee of power to budde."

The first time the current 'bud' version of the phrase is found in print is in 1607, in Beaumont and Fletcher's 'comedy of manners Woman Hater': "Yet I can frowne and nip a passion Euen in the bud."

"The Writing's on the Wall"

Meaning: said when there are clear signs that a situation is going to become very difficult or unpleasant.

Origin: this idiom comes from the Biblical story of 'Belshazzar's feast', Daniel 5:5–31.

In the story, King Belshazzar witnessed a disembodied handwriting text he did not understand on the palace wall. The queen suggested he call Daniel to translate, and the king offered him a reward if he could interpret the writing.

Daniel told the king to keep the reward, but he would interpret the writing for the king, the message was a warning: "Mene, Mene, Tekel, Upharsin," meaning thy kingdom is divided, and will be given to the Medes and Persians.

The King ignored the message, and that night King Belshazzar was slain and Darius the Median took the kingdom. The king had 'seen the writing on the wall' but had not paid attention.

'Writing on the wall' began to be used figuratively from the early eighteenth century and the first example found in print with the saying as it is today is in Jonathan Swift's 'Miscellaneous works', 1720: "A baited banker thus desponds, from his own Hand foresees his Fall, they have his Soul who have his bonds, Tis like the Writing on the Wall."

"At Face Value"

Meaning: true or genuine without being questioned or doubted.

Origin: The origin of this saying is believed to have its roots in money. Several etymology sources make the same claim in that you can believe something as how you see it. With money, the value is clear as it is printed on the front of a note.

Some etymologists claim the face is relevant in this saying in that coins and notes have had Kings and Queens faces on them for centuries but there is no evidence of this.

What seems to not be in doubt is that the 'face' or display of value on money is not in question and that is where the saying 'at face value' comes from.

Though thought to be much older, the saying itself cannot be found in print prior to 1842.

"Keep Your Nose to the Grindstone"

Meaning: to work hard or diligently on something.

Origin: This phrase comes from the practice of knife grinders sharpening blades. Tool sharpening workshops would have benches where knife grinders would sit hunched over grinding stones.

They had to pay close attention to their work as a moment too long on the wheel could cause the steel to overheat and be ruined. These knife grinders therefore would literally have their noses next to the grindstone and it was known as very arduous work.

The first the phrase can be seen in print is in John Frith's 'A Mirrour or Glasse to know thyselfe', 1532: "This Text holdeth their noses so hard to the grindstone, that it clean disfigureth their faces."

The phrase has since come to be used as an analogy for any kind of hard work.

"Wheeler Dealer"

Meaning: a person who engages in commercial or political scheming.

Origin: Etymologists believe the origin of this term lies in the early eighteenth century American West. A big wheeler and dealer was known at this time to be a heavy better on cards and roulette wheels at this time.

The more negative connotation and more recent meaning of a 'wheeler-dealer', meaning a conman, seems to have come a little later and specifically seems to originate within the motor trade. We can see advertisers in 1930s America offering 'Wheel deals' for car sales.

Still not particularly derogatory at this point, but fast forward another 30 years and we can see the term moving from the vehicle to those selling the vehicle in a negative manner. The 1960 'Wentworth and Flexner's Dictionary of American slang' describes a wheeler dealer as 'an adroit, quick-witted, scheming person'.

So although the term is originally seen attached to gambling, the negative and more recent connotation seems to have come from the car sales industry and the opinion of 'wheeler dealer' seems to have turned sour, presumably from numerous bad deals being spotlighted somewhere in the late 1950s, as positive examples of the term can be seen as late as 1954.

"The Grass Is Always Greener on the Other Side"

Meaning: used to say that the things a person does not have always seem more appealing than the things he or she does have.

Origin: This saying is thought to be very old indeed and Etymologists believe it has developed from the writings of ancient Roman poet, Ovid.

Translated in 1885 by Henry T.Riley, Ovid's 'Book of love' wrote around 2AD reads the following: "The crop of corn is always more fertile in the fields of other people; and the herds of our neighbours have their udders more distended."

In 1545, we see Dutch philosopher, Desiderius Erasmus Roterodamus write "The corne in an other man's ground semeth euer more fertyll and plentifull then doth oure own."

Still not the exact saying we see today but the theme is the same, yearning for what one does not have. It is not until much later we see the saying as we see it today. The first it can be found in print is in 1897 in Pennsylvania paper 'The Public Press': "The mines are wonderful, but probably not so wonderful as represented. Grass is always greener, you know, further away."

Throughout all versions of the proverb are pointers in the direction of the lesson of being satisfied with what one has rather than wanting what another has.

"Take a Rain Check"

Meaning: politely decline an offer, with the implication that one may take it up at a later date.

Origin: This term originates in America and can be found in the late nineteenth century in relation to baseball. The 'Check' in question here is a ticket for a baseball game.

If someone had purchased a ticket for a baseball game and the game was postponed due to poor weather, the ticket holder could come back to watch another game.

This is something that was formalised by famous Baseball player, manager and then owner of numerous teams, Abner Powell, when he was a member of the Nationals of the Union Association in 1889.

More recently we use 'rain check' in a looser fashion to suggest that an offer will be taken up at a later date, although it is frequently also used as a politer alternative to turning someone down.

"Hang Fire"

Meaning: delay or be delayed in taking action or progressing.

Origin: This phrase originates in the sixteenth century when flintlock firearms were loaded using a gunpowder charge poured from a flask, which was then ignited by a spark from a flint striking against an iron plate.

Gunpowder was notoriously unreliable, based on the quality or damp stopping it igniting properly. If this happened, the powder smouldered but did not explode and was said to 'hang fire'.

To 'hang fire' became an expression used figuratively for an event that was slow or a person hesitating, usually with the inference that a matter of some importance was to follow. The phrase in the figurative sense can be seen in print several times but much later in the late eighteenth century.

"A Load of Baloney"

Meaning: nonsense, foolishness or poor quality.

Origin: Boloney or Baloney is an American English alteration of Bologna sausage. The sausage was first made in the Italian City of Bologna, hence the name, and is a sausage historically made of leftover scraps of different blended meats, therefore of dubious quality.

The figurative use of the word meaning poor quality can be seen in the early 1920s in relation to unskilled fighters in the sport of boxing.

The Bologna sausage can be seen referenced in print many times in the 1800s but the first the figurative version of boloney can be seen in print is in New York newspaper 'The Evening World', 1922: "Promising Oasis Yields Only a 'Lot of Boloney'."

"Rain on Someone's Parade"

Meaning: to spoil someone's pleasure.

Origin: The term 'To rain on one's parade' started to appear in the early twentieth century although there is no specific 'Parade' we can track the saying specifically too.

The first the term can be seen is in the figurative sense and is first seen in print in the New York paper, the 'Schenectady Gazette', 1912: "Warmbody says he knew dog-gon well, some gosh-blamed leftover-from-the-summer hen would show up to rain on the parade."

The term was further popularised in the 1963 musical and movie 'Funny Girl' where the song 'Don't rain on my parade' is seen.

The term has evolved and there are many modern slangs terms that have evolved from it, a popular one in the UK is 'don't p**s on my bonfire/chips'.

"Play Devil's Advocate"

Meaning: a person who expresses a contentious opinion in order to provoke debate or test the strength of the opposing arguments.

Origin: The canonisation process, which is the process of deciding whether to make someone a saint, historically involved employing some decision makers. There were three decision makers:

- 'The Promoter of the Faith', who represented the Catholic church.
- 'The Devil's Advocate', who's role was to take a sceptical view of the candidate's character and look for flaws or holes in the reason for bestowing Sainthood on an individual.
- 'God's Advocate', also known as 'The promoter of the cause', whose role was to argue in favour of the canonisation. 'The Promoter of the Faith' is still a congregational figure to this day.

This employment of these officers seems to have been formally established in 1587, during the reign of Pope Sixtus V although the first formal mention of 'The Devil's Advocate' officer is found in the canonisation of St Lawrence Justinian under Pope Leo X (1513–1521).

Pope John Paul II reduced the power of these officers and changed the role of the office in 1983.

"Stick Your Neck Out"

Meaning: risk incurring criticism or anger by acting or speaking boldly.

Origin: Though not definitive, some etymologists believe this phrase goes back as far as Shakespeare's time as a very similar phrase is used in 'Henry V', 1599: "Fluellen, thinking the soldier Williams has done a traitorous thing, says, 'Let his neck answer for it'."

This would be a very logical origin as public executions would have been common at the time and 'sticking one's neck out' might be quite the risk in the era of hanging and the guillotine however there is no conclusive proof and there are other theories.

The exact phrase 'Stick your neck out' in the form we see it today is not seen in print until the 1960s in America where it is listed as slang for taking a risk.

Many believe the phrase is based on the barnyard chicken that was laid on a chopping block with its neck stretched out and then beheaded with an axe and there is a theory which relates to turtle's sticking their necks out and becoming more vulnerable to predators.

I will leave you to decide which you find more likely.

"Stake Your Claim"

Meaning: indicate something as one's own.

Origin: This expression has its origins in the California gold rush of 1848–1855.

At its height in 1849, up to 300,000 prospectors were thought to have embarked on California and this expression refers to the practice of putting **stakes** around the perimeter of a piece of land to which a **claim** is laid by a prospector.

The claim being that this area was theirs as they had discovered it first and they alone could mine for gold in this area.

The expression has since come to be used figuratively for anyone claiming ownership of anything.

"Ivory Tower"

Meaning: a state of privileged seclusion or separation from the facts and practicalities of the real world.

Origin: The origin of this one lies in the King James version of the Bible, in the 'song of Solomon', 7:4: "Thy neck is as a tower of ivory; thine eyes like the fishpools in Heshbon." The Biblical story is an allusion that the ivory towers are a symbol of virginal purity.

The ivory towers are mentioned numerous times in print from the eighteenth century but the first time the figurative meaning can be found in print is in the collaborative work of Frederick Rothwell and Cloudesley Shovell Henry Brereton's text, '*H. L. Bergson's Laughter*', 1911: "Each member of society must be ever attentive to his social surroundings, he must avoid shutting himself up in his own peculiar character as a philosopher in his ivory tower."

"Halloween"

Meaning: all Hallows Eve.

Origin: The traditions of Halloween are older than you think. Although the festivities we see today are very different from the traditions in which it is believed they started.

The Celts, based in what is now Ireland, The UK and Northern France celebrated a pre-Christian festival more than 2000 years ago called 'Samhain' around this time of year.

During 'Samhain' festivals the Celts would wear costumes made of animal skins to drive spirits away as they believed this night, thought to be October 31st or around this time, the dead returned to earth.

Historians believe similar traditions continued but changed over time as religion changed and around 609AD Pope Gregory III designated November 1 as a time to honour all saints. Shortly after 'All Saints Day' incorporated some of the traditions of Samhain. The evening before was known as All Hallows Evening or Eve, and later Halloween.

"Hand Over Fist"

Meaning: quickly and in large amounts – usually in making money.

Origin: This term has a nautical history. The allusion in this phrase is to the action of hauling on a rope. An earlier version of the phrase was 'hand over hand', which dates to the mid-eighteenth century.

This first 'hand over hand' is seen in print is in a paper by Cooke in the 'Royal Society's Philosophical Transactions', 1736: "A lusty young man attempted to go down (hand over hand, as the Workmen call it) by means of a single rope."

The more modern term, 'Hand over fist', is first seen in print in William Glascock's 'The naval sketchbook', 1825: "The French...weathered our wake, coming up with us, 'hand over fist', in three divisions."

Although the term is now used to suggest speed, for example, 'making money, hand over fist', the earlier term meant to make steady progress.

"Cry Me a River"

Meaning: said sarcastically when one feels another is being overly dramatic.

Origin: 'Cry me a river' was a song written by Arthur Hamilton in 1955 and recorded by Julie London and Ella Fitzgerald. It is not seen in print before this and Hamilton said that he had never heard the phrase before. He thought that it was an interesting way to get his message across.

The famous lyrics went as follows: "Now you say you're lonely, you cried the long night through. Well, you can cry me a river, Cry me a river, I cried a river over you."

The use of the term in the unsympathetic sarcastic tone it is used today gained notoriety when it was submitted to the urban dictionary in 2003 following Justin Timberlake's hit song by the same name the prior year.

"Throw Caution to the Wind"

Meaning: act in a completely reckless manner.

Origin: The first time this saying can be seen in print is in a prayer by religious writer Richard Rolle, there is no date on the prayer, but Rolle died in 1349. The line reads as follows: "Desire for you that is unrestrained and a yearning for you that throws caution to the winds, and this for your own love's sake. Amen."

It is likely the line is understood at this point for it to be in this writing, but it is not certain that the meaning is the same.

Three hundred years later, we see the saying 'Throw discretion to the winds', and the meaning at this point was to behave or speak very rashly. *'To the winds'* is used in the sense of 'utterly vanishing' or 'out of existence', and this figurative meaning can be tracked back in print to the early 1600s.

'Throw caution to the wind' seems to come a little later and seems to have the same figurative meaning. The first it can be found in print is in English poet John Milton's 'Paradise Lost', no definitive date but Milton died 1674: "And fear of Death deliver to the windes."

Although we cannot be certain of the exact origin of the saying, what we can say is that the line has been used for at least 700 years.

"Not Worth a Bean"

Meaning: worthless.

Origin: Beans have been considered a cheap and readily available food source for many centuries and this saying is at least 700 years old.

The first the phrase can be seen in print is in Robert Gloucester's 'English chronicles', 1297. A little later in 1380, we see Chaucer, Troilus and Criseyde write: "Swich arguments ne been nat worth a bene."

The phrase has been adopted by Americans, Australians, South Africans and Indians and seems to be used wherever British travellers have settled in other countries from the 1700s.

"Safe and Sound"

Meaning: unharmed and free from injury.

Origin: This phrase is very old, and we see 'sound' being used in Middle English around the beginning of the fourteenth century. The saying meant the same back then as the secondary definition of sound means today – 'whole, not damaged or injured'. The 'safe' part of the phrase speaks for itself and has always been used in the same way.

The first time we see the full phrase in print is not until 1594 in William Shakespeare's play 'The comedy of errors': "Fetch our stuff from thence: I long that we were safe and sound aboard."

"Under the Weather"

Meaning: slightly unwell or in low spirits.

Origin: This term has nautical origins and is thought to refer to sailors feeling seasick. The original term was 'under the weather bow' which is thought to indicate the side of the boat where the poor weather was.

The saying is quite logical in that sailors became seasick usually because of the boat rocking due to choppy waters caused by storms or bad weather. When someone became sick on the boat, they would be sent below deck and would therefore literally be under the weather.

The term quickly became used figuratively meaning 'feeling sick' in any scenario, not just on boats and the first time it can be found in print in this way is in the '*Jeffersonville Daily* Evening News', 1835: "I own Jessica is somewhat under the weather today, figuratively and literally," said the gentleman, amusedly, giving a glance at the lady over in the corner.

"You Can't Have Your Cake and Eat It"

Meaning: you can't enjoy both of two desirables but mutually exclusive alternatives.

Origin: This popular phrase has been around for centuries, and cakes have been around for even longer, cakes date back to the Egyptian times, but in the UK, where the phrase is first recorded, cakes have been recognised as far back as the thirteenth century.

The phrase itself can be first seen in print in John Heywood's glossary 'A Dialogue conteinyng the number in effect of all the Prouerbes in the Englishe tongue', 1546: "Wolde ye bothe eate your cake, and haue your cake."

The phrase meant the same back then and was used figuratively in the Tudor era, just as it is today, meaning you can't have everything you want.

"Dutch Courage"

Meaning: strength or confidence gained from drinking alcohol.

Origin: The etymology of the term Dutch courage relates to English soldiers fighting in the Anglo-Dutch Wars (1652–1674) and perhaps as early as the Thirty Years' War (1618–1648).

Jenever (or Dutch gin) was used by English soldiers for its calming effects before battle, and for its purported warming properties on the body in cold weather. It is also said English soldiers noted the bravery-inducing effects of jenever on Dutch soldiers in battle.

Gin, an English adaptation of jenever, would go on to become popular in Britain thanks to King William III of England (William of Orange, r. 1689–1702), who was also Stadtholder of the Netherlands.

Before anyone asks… I know Arnie is Austrian/American but his character in Predator is called…

"Dyed in the Wool"

Meaning: unchanging in a particular belief or opinion.

Origin: This idiom seems to have its origins in the literal sense of dyeing wool. Before modern machinery made the process much easier, dying wool was a manual task and the easiest way to make sure colour was consistent or unchanging was to dye the entire coat of wool in its raw form before it was made into yarn. The saying can be seen from the 1600s in the United Kingdom in the literal sense but not until much later in the figurative sense.

The concept of something being 'true' throughout seems to have been transferred to other forms of genuineness later and the first the figurative sense can be seen in print is in a speech by Daniel Webster, former United States Secretary of State, in 1830: "In half an hour, he can come out an original democrat, dyed in the wool." The idiom is presumably understood by this point however for a politician to be using the term in a speech.

"Face the Music"

Meaning: to accept the consequences or own up to the responsibility created by one's actions.

Origin: Not all Etymologists agree on the origin of this idiom and there are thought to be two possible explanations:

The first theory is that it is to do with stage fright and literally facing one's fears in the theatre, playing music or acting in front of a crowd and therefore 'facing the music' literally.

The other theory is based within the United States' military. During a ceremony when a disgraced soldier was ejected from the army a certain drum cadence was played, in essence that soldier would be facing the music. If this 'drumming out' process is the origin of the idiom, then this has been witnessed in print in first in the UK in 1731 and in the US in 1778.

Presumably, the figurative meaning has stemmed from a literal meaning and the first example of the figurative meaning can be seen in print in 'The New Hampshire Statesman & State Journal', 1834: "Will the editor of the Courier explain this black affair. We want no equivocation, 'face the music' this time."

I'll let you decide which origin you find more plausible.

"Fit as a Fiddle"

Meaning: in very good physical condition.

Origin: The 'fiddle' in question in this phrase is the colloquial name for a violin. 'Fit' didn't originally mean healthy and energetic, in the sense it is used today to describe regular visitors of the gymnasium.

The sole meaning of the word 'fit' initially meant suitable or adequate, in the way we still say 'fit for purpose'.

We see a very similar phrase in Thomas Dekker's 'The Batchelars Banquet', 1603: "Then comes downe mistresse Nurse as fine as a farthing fiddle, in her petticoate and kertle."

Shortly after 'fine as a fiddle' in W. Haughton's 'English-men for my Money' 1616, we see in print the modern phrase for the first time: "This is excellent in faith, as fit as a fiddle."

"Take Pot-Luck"

Meaning: a situation in which one must take a chance that whatever is available will prove to be good or acceptable.

Origin: This term now means to take your chances in a number of scenarios but was far more specific originally. To take 'Potluck' originally meant to blindly take the food provided in a pot provided by a host.

The term is used in most English-speaking countries but originated in the UK and can first be seen in print in Thomas Nashe's 'Strange newes', 1592: "That pure sanguine complexion of yours may neuer be famisht with potte-lucke."

In the sixteenth century, 'pot-luck' was almost always hyphenated, which points to an earlier time when it was written as two words. The ongoing effort to digitise old manuscripts may turn up a pre-sixteenth century 'potte lucke' – we'll just have to take our chance on that.

The American 'bring food to a party' meaning was defined in an entry in American Speech in 1924: "Potluck, food contributed by the guest. To take potluck is to bring food with one to a party."

"Keep Your Hair On"

Meaning: used to urge someone not to panic or lose their temper.

Origin: There is no definitive origin for this one and etymologists disagree on its roots (pun intended).

The first theory is that it is in reference to the era where lords and ladies wore powdered wigs, starting in the mid-seventeenth century. An angry lord or lady may show their 'cool' by keeping their wigs on.

The second theory is that it is in reference to an earlier phrase, 'Pulling my hair out', meaning someone is angry and therefore 'keeping one's hair on' is staying calm.

The final theory is that it is in reference to being scalped in the Wild West era of America.

Although the origin probably lies in the literal sense, the figurative sense can first be seen in print in 1873 in a London Music Hall production where an artist by the name of Ted Callingham performs a comical song named 'Keep your hair on'.

One would assume for it to be the title of a song, the phrase is understood by this point, and we see the phrase being used in America, New Zealand and Australia shortly after.

"The Nature of the Beast"

Meaning: the inherent and unchangeable character of something.

Origin: All old writings show that this idiom was originally about the nature of an animal rather than the 'Beast' in this saying meaning the devil. Originally this phrase meant that you cannot change the ways of a wild animal as it is 'The nature of the beast' to behave in a set way.

It appears in a literal sense at least as early as the middle 1500s. This is the first recorded written example from a 1567 translation of Ovid's Metamorphosis by Arthur Golding: "The nature of the beast that dooth delyght in bloody food."

We see 'the nature of the beast' in allusion to the devil first in David Pareus, 'A Commentary upon the Divine Revelation of the Apostle and Evangelist Iohn' (1644): "Such indeed are blasphemers out of the Church. But principally it agrees to the worshippers of the Beast, for they imitate the nature of the Beast."

The saying has since come to mean the nature or character of anything, man or beast.

"Every Cloud Has a Silver Lining"

Meaning: a negative occurrence may have a positive aspect to it.

Origin: This expression can be traced directly from a piece written by English poet John Milton called 'Comus: A Mask Presented at Ludlow Castle', 1634: "Was I deceived or did a sable cloud Turn forth her silver lining on the night?"

We see several mentions of 'silver linings' being mentioned after this and references of 'Milton's clouds' but it is not until the Victorian era that we see the expression used as it is today.

The first time we see it in print is in 'The Dublin magazine' in a review of a novel called 'Marian, a young maids fortunes' 1840: "There's a silver lining to every cloud that sails about the heavens if we could only see it."

"Dark Horse"

Meaning: a contestant that on paper should be unlikely to succeed but yet still might.

Origin: The term began as horse racing parlance for a racehorse that is unknown to gamblers and thus difficult to place betting odds on.

The first known mention of the concept is in Benjamin Disraeli's novel 'The Young Duke', 1831. Disraeli's protagonist, the Duke of St James, attends a horse race with a surprise finish: "A dark horse which had never been thought of, and which the careless St James had never even observed in the list, rushed past the grandstand in sweeping triumph."

The term later became used figuratively for any candidate, sporting or otherwise, whom little is known about but may unexpectedly win or succeed.

"Between a Rock and a Hard Place"

Meaning: being faced with a dilemma that only affords a choice between two unpleasant alternatives.

Origin: Throughout history, there have been numerous sayings with similar meanings, in that neither available choice is particularly attractive. Other examples are 'the lesser of two evils', 'between the devil and the deep blue sea', 'an offer you can't refuse' and 'Hobson's choice'.

Etymologists believe 'Between a rock and a hard place' specifically originated in America in the early 1900s to describe a dispute between copper miners and the mining companies in Bisbee, Arizona. The miners demanded better working conditions, which the companies refused to supply.

The miners were left with two unpleasant choices: continue to mine in the same terrible conditions (a rock), or face unemployment and poverty (a hard place). The phrase came into popular use during The Great Depression of the 1930s, as many citizens found themselves caught between a rock and a hard place.

The first time it can be seen in print is in the American Dialect Society's publication Dialect Notes V, 1921: "To be between a rock and a hard place, to be bankrupt. Common in Arizona in recent panics and sporadic in California."

"Another Day Another Dollar"

Meaning: a resignation that the day to come will be tedious work, the only benefit being the small amount of payment at the end of it.

Origin: This expression is thought to date from the days when sailors were paid a dollar a day in the USA in the nineteenth century. On long voyages, each day was similar to the last and all that the seamen had to show for a day's work was one more dollar in their pocket.

Joseph Conrad referred to the form of payment in his seafaring novel, 'The Narcissus: A Tale of the Forecastle', 1897: "The common saying, 'More days, more dollars', did not give the usual comfort because the stores were running short."

The currently used form of the expression soon started appearing in other places and is first seen in print in a story entitled 'Gittin' up time', excerpts of which can be found in the Indiana newspaper 'The Logansport Daily Reporter', 1907: "I sat up and stretched and yawned. Oh hum! The same old grind. Another day, another dollar."

The expression has long since lost its nautical connections and is now used worldwide as an ironic and weary resignation of marking the start of another unremarkable working day.

The expression was popularised in a song of the same name that was recorded in 1962 by Wynn Stewart at the Capitol Recording Studio, located in Hollywood, California.

"Barking Up the Wrong Tree"

Meaning: pursuing a mistaken or misguided line of thought or course of action.

Origin: The origin of this one is quite simple; it is an allusion to hunting dogs tracking animals to the wrong location.

This one seems to be of American origin and was used literally in the very early 1800s. The figurative version seems to have come along roughly 30 years later and the earliest example found in print is in James Kirke Paulding's 'Westward Ho', 1832: "I thought I'd set him barking up the wrong tree a little, and I told him some stories that were enough to set the Mississippi a-fire, but he put them all down in his book."

Soon after Paulding's work, we see it appear in several American newspapers throughout the late 1830s.

"Born With a Silver Spoon in One's Mouth"

Meaning: be born into a wealthy family of high social standing.

Origin: This phrase is thought to originate in the UK and is thought to refer to British aristocracy. It has been a tradition in many countries for godparents of the wealthy to give children a silver spoon at christening ceremonies and this is thought to be where the phrase originates.

The first time we see the phrase in print in English is in Peter Anthony Motteux's translation of the novel 'Don Quixote', 1719: "Mum, Teresa, quoth Sancho, 'tis not all gold that glisters, and every man was not born with a Silver Spoon in his Mouth."

This however alludes to an even earlier origin as Spanish writer Miguel de Cervantes novel 'Don Quixote' was originally published 1605–1615 in Spain and was later translated, although the phrase does not translate directly into English.

Either way, although the saying itself may be English, its origins lie in Spain it would seem.

"Train of Thought"

Meaning: the way in which someone reaches a conclusion or a line of reasoning.

Origin: This phrase is actually older than trains (as in the transportation vehicle) themselves. The railway system of Great Britain started with the building of local isolated wooden wagonways starting in the 1560s but at this time there were no trains. Trains as we know them did not come along until the 1800s and yet this phrase can be seen in the mid-seventeenth century.

The first recorded use of *'train of thought'* was in 1651, in a book called 'Leviathan' by Thomas Hobbes, and is explained as *'train'* meaning a series or progression.

In the book, it is described as a train in the sense of an orderly sequence: "By consequence, or train of thoughts, I understand that succession of one thought to another which is called, to distinguish it from discourse in words, mental discourse."

"The Final Straw"

Meaning: the last in a series of bad things that happen to make someone very upset, angry.

Origin: 'The final straw' is a shortened version of the metaphorical phrase 'The last straw which breaks the camel's back'. The Oxford Dictionary of Quotations dates the full phrase to the mid-1600s though there is no evidence of this.

The earliest it can be found in print is in newspaper, 'The Edinburgh Advertiser', 1816: "Straw upon straw was laid till the last straw broke the camel's back."

Camels haven't always been the subject of the figurative abuse however as in the same newspaper in 1829 we see the following text: "Agitation was only the cause of Emancipation in the same sense in which it is true that the last feather breaks the horse's back."

To further confuse matters we see a merger of the two phrases in newspaper, 'The Southport American' in October 1843: "And finally, the 'feather which breaks the camel's back' having been added to Sir Walter's burthen."

What we can say for sure is 'The final straw' originates from the longer saying involving a camel, the phrase is at least 200 years old and that the camels with straws won the race against Horses with feathers.

In the more modern era, we see numerous similar phrases such as 'Getting on one's wick', 'Putting the final nail in the coffin' and 'Getting on one's last nerve'.

"By the Skin of One's Teeth"

Meaning: a situation from which one has barely managed to escape or achieve something.

Origin: The phrase by the skin of one's teeth is first found in print 'the book of Job' in the Old Testament of the Bible, 1560. Job is a character in the Bible who undergoes an abundance of suffering due to a challenge that Satan has made to God.

Satan tries to break Job's righteousness by bringing suffering upon him. Job laments his status through much of the book, including the phrase, "My bone cleaveth to my skin and to my flesh, and I am escaped with the skin of my teeth."

What exactly the phrase 'escaped with the skin of my teeth' meant in Ancient Hebrew is not certain but it is assumed that the skin referred to in the term is the enamel on one's teeth.

"Once in a Blue Moon"

Meaning: very rarely.

Origin: On very rare occasions, the moon does actually appear blue. One phenomenon that can make this happen is after a volcanic eruption, in these areas, particles in the air dependent on their size can make the moon look either blue or red.

This however is not thought to be the source of the phrase, originally the phrase did not mean unlikely, it meant impossible, and was used as a source of sarcasm or ridicule.

The earliest example of this found in print is in 'The Treatyse of the Buryall of the Masse' by William Barlow, the Bishop of Chichester, 1528: "Yf they saye the mone is belewe, we must beleve that it is true."

It is not until centuries later we see the 'unlikely' meaning of blue moon appear and it is credited to an American amateur astronomer called James Pruett.

In America, since 1819, The Maine Farmers' Almanac has listed the dates of forthcoming 'blue moons'. Lunar and calendar months are not exactly the same, most years we see 12 full moons a year, but every 3rd year we see 13 full moons.

The compilers of the almanac have names for these full moons, the common ones we see such as 'Harvest moon, and 'Hunters moon' are part of the normal 12 moon year.

The afore mentioned James Pruett read the almanac and mistakenly named the 13th moon 'The blue moon' in a 1946 version of 'Sky and telescope' magazine. It is thought to have stuck as his incorrect version appeared as an answer in an early version of the game 'Trivial Pursuit' and came into common usage from this time.

"Rome Wasn't Built in a Day"

Meaning: a complex task or great achievement takes time and effort and should not be rushed.

Origin: Why Rome? Why not Paris, London or Madrid? Etymologists believe the age of the saying is the answer to this question.

This saying is very old and yet cannot be found first in Latin, but in French. The first known reference of the saying is by a cleric in the court of Phillippe of Alsace, the Count of Flanders, in present-day Belgium, in a book of poems called 'Li Proverbe au Vilain', 1190: "Rome ne fu pas faite toute en un jour', which translates in English to 'Rome was not built in just one day'."

It is thought in this era Rome, 'The Eternal City' would have been revered as the greatest City in history, With its layers of stunning architecture, embarrassment of artistic masterpieces and countless ancient treasures.

The saying is first seen in print in English in Richard Taverner's translation from the Latin of Desiderius Erasmus's work, 'adages' 1545: "one daye is not ynoughe for acheuinge a great matter, Rome was not buylt in one day."

The popularity of the saying increased dramatically when famous English writer, John Heywood, listed the proverb in his work 'A Dialogue conteinyng the nomber in effect of all the Prouerbes in the Englishe tongue', 1546: "Rome was not bylt on a daie and yet stood Tyll it was fynysht."

The proverb was well enough known for Queen Elizabeth I to have included it in a public address that she made on a visit to Cambridge in 1564: "But this common saying has given me a certain amount of comfort – a saying which cannot take away, but can at least lessen, the grief that I feel; and the saying is, that Rome was not built in one day."

Much more recently the saying has been popularised in a 1962 soul song by Johnnie Taylor and a 2000 song by electronic band Morcheeba.

"Saving For a Rainy Day"

Meaning: put something aside for a future time of need.

Origin: This saying is very old and can be seen in print as early as 1580, when it was put as follows in 'The Bugbears': "Wold he haue me kepe nothing against a raynye day?"

But why save for a 'rainy day'? It's not certain, but experts believe 500 years ago a 'rainy day' could be calamitous for many workers such as farmers or smiths as they needed finer weather to be able to conduct their duties and therefore poor weather meant not getting paid.

The philosopher Abraham Tucker summed it up in the eighteenth century with the warning: "It behoves us to provide against a rainy day while the sun shines." A nod to a similar idiom, 'make hay while the sun shines', which advises us to seize the day while opportunity lasts, because rain will surely follow.

"A Stone's Throw"

Meaning: a short distance.

Origin: There have been a few variations of this phrase but the first with the same meaning can be seen in 'Wycliffe's Bible, Luke 22:41', 1526: "in nd he gat himself from them, about a stone's cast."

The first time we see the term in its current form is in Arthur Hall's translation of 'The Ten books of Homers Iliades'1581: "For who can see a stone's throw of ought thing in land or plaine?"

Other thrown objects were used to describe a short distance soon after, one example being the following from Nicholas Lichefield (1680–1750) wrote: "The enimyes were come, within the throwe of a Dart." Another example can be seen in Jonathan Swift's 'The battle of the books', 1704: "The two Cavaliers had now approach'd within a Throw of a Lance."

The 'stone's throw' variant won through and this is credited to John Arbuthnot's popular story 'The History of John Bull', 1712: "In spite of all applications the patient grew worse every day, she stunk so, nobody durst come within a stone's throw of her, except those quacks who attended her close, and apprehended no danger."

Several examples can be seen following this.

"Let One's Hair Down"

Meaning: behave uninhibitedly.

Origin: Etymologists believe this phrase has its roots (pardon the pun) in seventeenth century England. At this time, nobles, particularly ladies when in public would have their hair pinned up in particularly elaborate ways. Hair would be decorated with feathers or flowers and would sometimes have displays as high as two feet tall on top of their heads.

The term for taking off these ornate displays of hair at the time was dishevelling and it was done in the privacy of one's home when one could relax. These days, describing someone as dishevelled would create the image of someone unkempt or untidy but then it applied specifically to hair which was unpinned.

The first example of this found in print is in John Cotgrave's 'The English treasury of wit and language', 1655: "Descheveler, to discheuell; to pull the haire about the eares."

The phrase has taken numerous guises on the way to becoming the figurative way we use it today, in the sense of being able to relax.

The saying moved to 'letting one's back hair down' by the 1800s, referring to a ladies long hair being let over the shoulders. The first example found in print of this is in 'The United States Democratic Review', 1847: "Why do crazy women in operas always let their back hair down?"

By the 1920s, 'Letting one's back hair down' was being used figuratively meaning to relax and this can be seen numerous times in this era as it is being used as examples of men relaxing aswell as women.

It is not until much more recently we see the term used in it's current guise, the first example of this found in print is in 'Nones' by Auden, 1951: "To let their hair down and be frank about the world."

"A Bird in the Hand Is Worth Two in the Bush"

Meaning: it is better to hold onto something one has than to risk losing it by trying to get something better.

Origin: Etymologists believe this phrase is an allusion to falconry, where a bird in the hand (the falcon) was a valuable asset and worth more than two in the bush (the prey).

There are numerous variations of this phrase throughout history in multiple languages. The earliest variation is a fifth century papyri Egyptian translation, translated from ancient Aramaic, it reads: "Better is a bird held tight in the hand than a thousand birds flying about in the air."

Other languages also have their own variations, translated in Czech, we see "A sparrow in the fist is better than a pigeon on the roof." And in German, we see "The sparrow in the hand is better than the dove on the roof."

The first English written variation we see is in John Capgrave's 'The Life of St Katharine of Alexandria', 1450: "It is more certain a byrd in your fist, than to have three in the sky above."

A little later we see another variation in John Heywood's glossary 'A Dialogue conteinyng the number in effect of all the Prouerbes in the Englishe tongue' 1546: also includes a variant of the proverb: "Better one byrde in hande than ten in the wood." Due to Heywood's prominence, he is credited as introducing the proverb to the English language, but history tells the tale that his is a variation of older proverbs.

By the 1700s, 'A bird in the hand is worth two in the bush' has become the established version and this is seen throughout the English-speaking world at this time. In 1734, English migrants in Pennsylvania name a small town by the phrase.

In England, in the Middle Ages, many pubs are named after the proverb, usually a shortened version, 'The bird in the hand', and many still have the name to this day.

"Blowing Smoke Up Someone's Ass"

Meaning: lie to someone to flatter them or inflate their ego.

Origin: Believe it or not, a tobacco enema was a mainstream medical practice, in the late 1700s, doctors literally blew smoke up people's rectums.

It was a practice used to resuscitate people who were otherwise presumed dead. It was such a commonly used resuscitation method for drowning victims in particular, that the equipment used in this procedure was hung alongside certain major waterways in the United Kingdom. People frequenting waterways were expected to know the location of this equipment similar to modern times concerning the location of defibrillators.

Thankfully, this method was proved to not work by the 1800s.

Many believe this is where the phrase comes from, however etymologists do not agree. The time of this medical practice versus the usage of the phrase itself points towards the 'smoke' in question meaning false or lies, in the same way we understand another phrase, 'Smoke and mirrors', that is also commonly used in the time we first start to see the phrase.

The first time we see the phrase in print is much more recently in the Elliot Chase's book 'Tiger in the honeysuckle', 1965: "I knew you didn't call me in here to blow smoke up my ass." It is assumed the phrase is already in use for it to be understood in a novel but certainly seems to be a mid-1900s phrase rather than the 1700s when the medical practice was around.

"Costs an Arm and a Leg"

Meaning: something extremely expensive.

Origin: Though there is no definitive origin of this phrase, etymologists believe based on when it is first seen in print that the likelihood is it is a reference to the high cost paid by soldiers who suffered amputations in the 2nd world war.

The phrase is first seen figuratively in print in American paper 'The Long Beach Independent', 1949: "Food Editor Beulah Karney has more than 10 ideas for the homemaker who wants to say 'Merry Christmas' and not have it cost her an arm and a leg."

Presumably, the phrase is understood at this point for it to be in print at this time and this is just four years after the war finished.

It is believed the expression derived from an earlier phrase, 'I would give my right arm for' and the earliest example found in print of this is found in 'Sharpe's London Journal', 1849: "He felt as if he could gladly give his right arm to be cut off if it would make him, at once, old enough to go and earn money instead of Lizzy."

"Don't Count Your Chickens Before They Hatch"

Meaning: avoid any hastiness when evaluating the assets you have available.

Origin: This one is a simple one and means the same today as it did 450 years ago when it is first seen in print. It is a direct reference to the fact that eggs sometimes fail to hatch, reducing the number of live chicks in a clutch.

The first printed example is seen in London in work by Thomas Howell, 'New Sonnets and Pretty Pamphlets', 1570: "Count not they chickens that unhatched be, weigh words as wind till though find certainty."

The phrase is presumably even older than this as it is in print by this point and clearly understood. The phrase is seen numerous times after this and is famously captured by popular English poet Samuel Butler in the narrative poem 'Hudibras', 1664: "To swallow gudgeons ere they're catch'd, and count their chickens 'ere they're hatched."

"Not Worth One's Salt"

Meaning: not good value, usually in the context of payment to a person not being worth the service one receives from them.

Origin: Salt, or sodium chloride is essential in life, but was even more valuable many years ago. Before more modern methods, using salt was the primary method of preserving food, so unsurprisingly throughout history it has been seen as valuable.

The old latin word, sal, meaning salt is where the word salary has derived, again further evidence of salts value. Roman soldiers were actually paid in part salt as they were expected to buy their own goods and the salt was deducted from their pay as part of their overall wage.

Salt continued to be valuable throughout all generations, spawning other common sayings such as 'take it with a grain of salt' and 'salt of the earth'.

Etymologists believe this deep ingrained value of salt is where the phrase comes from which would allude to it being a very old phrase but actually it is much more modern than other similar phrases such as 'worth one's weight in gold' which can be seen in the fifteenth century.

The earliest it can be found in print is in 'The African Memoranda', a report of an expedition to Guinea Bissau, by Philip Beaver, 1805: "Hayles has been my most useful man, but of late not worth his salt."

"Skeletons in the Closet"

Meaning: a secret source of shame, potentially ruinous if exposed.

Origin: Though there is no proof, because of the timing of the usage of this phrase, many etymologists believe its origins derive from the era of the notorious body snatchers. Buried bodies were not considered property at this time and therefore could be exhumed and sold without restriction, though the practice was hated by the general public.

Prior to 1832, the UK's 'Anatomy act' allowed the use of corpses for medical research. Doctors had been known to conceal illegally held skeletons they used for teaching in cupboards.

The timing of the anatomy act and the first figurative use of the phrase itself in print also correlate, it can first be seen in UK monthly paper 'The Eclectic Review' in a piece by William Hendry Stowell, 1816: "Two great sources of distress are the danger of contagion and the apprehension of hereditary diseases. The dread of being the cause of misery to posterity has prevailed over men to conceal the skeleton in the closet."

The notion of a 'skeleton in the closet' as shorthand for the grim evidence of a murder was widely adopted into the language thanks to the writings of the popular Victorian author William Makepeace Thackeray.

Thackeray referred to 'a skeleton in every house' in a piece in 1845 and explicitly to 'skeletons in closets' in 'The Newcomes, memoirs of a most respectable family', 1855: "Some particulars regarding the Newcome family, which will show us that they have a skeleton or two in their closets, as well as their neighbours."

"Hocus Pocus"

Meaning: meaningless talk or activity, typically designed to fool someone or used by a person performing conjuring tricks.

Origin: Although the phrase 'Hocus Pocus' is now treated in a comedy fashion in relation to magic, similarly to other phrases like 'Abracadabra'(One I've covered previously) and Shazam, in the seventeenth century when the term is first used, 'magicians' could reasonably have expected that such exotic sounding phrases would fool some of the audience into believing that mysterious forces were being conjured up.

Magicians and conjurers were both revered and feared in this era, although those that were too convincing could be tried as witches so perhaps the wiser ones may air on the side of comedy juggling.

In 1634, a book entitled 'Hocus Pocus Junior – The Anatomy of Legerdemain' was printed. The author isn't named but it believed to have exerted significant influence on the literature of conjuring and magic tricks. The word 'Hocus Pocus' must already be understood for the book to be named after the phrase, but Etymologists believe the term will not predate the book by many decades.

Hocus is thought to be the source for the verb hoax. That doesn't appear until 1796 though and, although the link seems intuitive, there is no direct evidence to link the two words.

"Elbow Grease"

Meaning: energetic physical work needed to do or accomplish something.

Origin: There is no definitive origin of this expression, the most common story I have come across is that of a joke played on new apprentices, who are sent out to a shop to purchase 'Elbow grease'. Clearly this is a product that does not exist but there is no evidence to back this story.

In most of its earliest examples in print it seems to refer to the effort needed in cleaning things and it has long been said that the best sort of furniture polish is 'elbow grease', meaning there is no substitute for hard rubbing to create a polished shine.

The first the expression can be seen in print is in the English poet Andrew Marvell's 'Rehearsal Transpros'd', 1672: "Two or three brawny Fellows in a Corner, with meer Ink and Elbow grease, do more Harm than a Hundred systematical Divines with their sweaty Preaching."

A little later we see the term explained in the way it is used today, meaning hard work, in 'A New Dictionary of the Terms Ancient and Modern of the Canting Crew' 1699: "Elbow-grease, a derisory Term for Sweat."

The expression's inclusion in that particular dictionary, which itemises the language of the streets, suggests that it was a lower-class term.

We can see near identical terms in other countries. In French, we have 'huile de bras' or 'l'huile de coude', which translates as 'elbow oil' and in Danish we find 'knofedt', which translates as 'knuckle fat'.

"Crazy Like a Fox"

Meaning: seemingly foolish but actually very shrewd and cunning.

Origin: According to 'Etymonline', foxes being referred to as cunning, clever or sly dates back to roughly the twelfth century. It is believed this was because of their expertise as scavengers and the havoc they caused, particularly to poultrymen and farmers.

But why crazy? Again this is only based on the theory of etymologists but many believe rabies is the answer to this question, others suggest that some of the great droughts in America towards the end of the nineteenth century may have drove foxes into places they didn't normally frequent and this would fit with the timeline the phrase can first be seen.

The first time we can see the phrase in print metaphorically is in Peter B. Kyne's 'Captain Scraggs or the Green-Pea Pirates', 1911: "If old Scraggsy's crazy, he's crazy like a fox. What's rilin' him is the knowledge that he's stung to the heart an' can't admit it without at the same time admittin' he'd cooked up a deal to double-cross us."

The phrase is clearly in use very early twentieth century at least, but what seems to have rocketed its popularity is that it was the title of a book by popular American humourist S.J. Perelman, published in 1944.

Following this, the saying becomes even more mainstream with the popularity of the TV show by the same name which first screened in 1984.

"Last Ditch Effort"

Meaning: a final attempt to achieve something after all else has failed.

Origin: The origin of this phrase lies at the door of William of Orange (1650–1702), who is quoted as saying it in 1672 when declining the offer to be made Sovereign Prince of Holland in return for his capitulation to England and France.

William was at that time Stadholder of the Dutch Republic and became King of Great Britain and Ireland as William III in 1689.

Although There is no direct evidence of his use of the phrase he is quoted as using it by Bishop Burnet, who has written the King had said he used the term in the above dispute directly to himself.

It can be seen in print following his death in 'Bishop Burnet's History of his own time Volume I', 1724: "The Prince's answer deserves to be remembered. He said, he saw it was indeed in great danger, but there was a sure way never to see it lost, and that was to die in the last ditch."

But what ditch is he referring to? The ditches referred to are the trenches outside a castle, used to defend it. The last ditch would be the final trench before the castle could be breached, to die in it would be to fight until the end.

What we can say for sure is, whether fact or fiction, the story of William of Orange is the source of the saying. It cannot be seen used beforehand and can be seen multiple times from this point on.

"Keeping on the Straight and Narrow"

Meaning: to follow a morally upright or law abiding route through life.

Origin: The source of this expression is a simple one, it is directly taken from the King James version of the Bible, 1604: "Because strait is the gate, and narrow is the way, which leadeth unto life, and few there be that find it."

The complication comes when deciding if the expression should be 'straight' or 'strait', the reference in the bible uses 'strait' rather than 'straight' and is in relation to another meaning of the word; A route or channel, so narrow as to make passage difficult. This is still found in the names of various sea routes, e.g. the Straits of Dover.

We still use 'strait', meaning confined or restricted in other words/terms; strait jacket, strait laced or dire straits are some examples.

Before we start to question ourselves too much, both ways of saying the term are now accepted by the Oxford English Dictionary. The first time we see 'straight and narrow' in print is in 'The Critical Works of Monsieur Rapin', 1706: "The soul of the common people seems too straight and narrow to be wrought upon by any Part of Eloquence."

'Straight and narrow' is now the more common spelling and you will be in good company if you opt to use it, even though 'strait and narrow' might be a better choice if you want to get high marks in that English language test.

"A Different Kettle of Fish"

Meaning: an issue or matter that is entirely different from the one that is being discussed.

Origin: It is not certain why 'a kettle of fish' is chosen in this phrase but it is thought it was just an amusing way of saying another matter. There are other more modern similar expressions, such as that's 'another ball game'.

But what is a 'kettle of fish'? We think of the modern-day kettle as a device for making tea or coffee, but many years ago, fish kettles were used to poach fish and were much larger than the kettles we use to make a hot beverage. They were large saucepans and were big enough to put large live fish in them such as salmon.

The earliest example found in print of a fish kettle is found in an old cookery book by Hannah Glasse called 'The Art of Cookery, Made Plain and Easy', 1747: "To boil a Cod's Head. Set a fish kettle on the fire, with water enough to boil it, a good handful of salt, a pint of vinegar, a bundle of sweet herbs, and a piece of horse-radish."

Kettles of fish were put by freshwater and would be taken on a picnic to catch, poach and eat the fish as a treat when out. In 1785, Thomas Newte published 'A Tour in England and Scotland'. In this, he referred to fish kettles: "It is customary for the gentlemen who live near the Tweed to entertain their neighbours and friends with a picnic, which they call giving 'a kettle of fish'. Tents or marquees are pitched near the flowery banks of the river…a fire is kindled, and live salmon thrown into boiling kettles."

Another phrase, 'A pretty kettle of fish' can also be seen in this era, this though means a mess or sticky situation one might find themselves in.

"Beyond the Pale"

Meaning: outside the bounds of acceptable behaviour.

Origin: The first thing is to distinguish 'Pale' from 'pail' as the term is frequently misspelt. The phrase has nothing to do with buckets and should correctly be termed 'Beyond the pale'.

The 'Pale' used here also has nothing to do with a white or light colour either, and in fact refers to a pale, meaning a stake or pointed piece of wood. The term is virtually redundant now but can still be seen in 'Paling a fence' or to 'impale' something, as in something you may see in a vampire movie.

The paling fence is significant as the term 'pale' came to mean the area enclosed by such a fence and later just figuratively 'the area that is enclosed and safe'. So to be 'beyond the pale' was to be outside the area accepted as 'home'.

Catherine the Great famously created the Pale of Settlement in Russia in 1791. This was the name given to the western border region of the country, in which Jews were allowed to live. The motivation behind this was to restrict trade between Jews and native Russians. Some Jews were allowed to live, as a concession, 'beyond the pale'.

Pales were enforced in various other European countries prior to this for similar political reasons, notably in Ireland (the Pale of Dublin) and France (the Pale of Calais, which was formed as early as 1360).

The phrase itself originated later than that. The first printed reference comes in John Harington's poem 'The History of Polindor and Flostella', 1657: "Both Dove-like roved forth beyond the pale to planted Myrtle-walk."

"Underdog" and "Top Dog"

Meaning: an 'underdog' is a competitor thought to have little chance of winning a fight or contest whereas a top dog is a competitor in a position of authority or strong favourite to win.

Origin: Both 'Underdog' and 'Topdog' have the same origin hence me covering both terms in the same origin story.

Sadly, the origins of both come from the barbaric history of dog fighting and although dog fighting had existed for centuries before throughout the world, the terms themselves seem to stem from early to mid-nineteenth century America.

Betting on the outcomes of dog fights was very common from the early 1800s in America and was not outlawed until the late 1900s when police and animal control law enforcers forced the activity to go underground.

When placing a bet on the outcome, bookkeepers would offer better odds on the 'underdog' than the 'topdog'.

The first time we see the terms in print is in the work of American poet, David Barker, 1859: "But for me and I care not a single fig, if they say I am wrong or right wrong, I shall always go for the weaker dog, For the underdog in the fight. I know that the world, that the great big world, Will never a moment stop. To see which dog may be in the fault, but will shout for the dog on top."

People supporting the 'Underdog' became popular mainly because people would make more money on an 'underdog' bet than a 'topdog' bet and this quickly leaped to not just other 'sports' but any kind of competitive scenario.

The terms are both widely enough recognised to make the leap from literal to figurative meaning and the first time we see either term used in this way is in 'The speaker, a review of politics', 1900: "The most popular argument in favour of the war is that it will make the individual Briton top dog in South Africa."

The 'Underdog' figure became so popular that we see a 1960s cartoon character appear by the same name and this is thought to have popularised the 'Underdog' further.

"On Tenterhooks"

Meaning: to be in a state of uncomfortable suspense or impatience.

Origin: Tenterhooks, not to be mixed up with hooks used by butchers, known as 'tenderhooks'. Tenterhooks are hooks on a wooden frame used to hang woollen or linen cloth to prevent it from shrinking as it dries. The tenterhooks are the hooks on the tenter (the wooden frame) used to hold the cloth in place.

Centuries ago, in wool weaving areas like the North of England, they were a common sight on the land around the many woollen mills, called 'tenter-fields'. It is easy to see how the figurative expression 'on tenterhooks', with its meaning of painful tension, derived from the 'tenting' or stretching of fabric.

The expression was originally 'on the tenters'. The English West Country playwright John Ford was the first to record that expression in the play Broken Heart, 1633: "Passion, O, be contained. My very heart strings Are on the Tenters."

Towards the end of the century, the more accurate 'on the tenterhooks' began to replace the earlier phrase. This first example found of it in print is in 'The General History of Europe', 1690: "The mischief is, they will not meet again these two years, so that all business must hang upon the tenterhooks till then."

"Gobbledygook"

Meaning: language that is meaningless or is made unintelligible by excessive use of technical terms.

Origin: This one was a relatively simple one to find as it can be definitively traced to one man who created the word and explained why he named it so.

Democratic congressman and Mayor of San Antonio, Maury Maverick, created the term gobbledygook. Whilst working in the House of Representatives, supporting the smaller war plants corporation who were supporting the efforts of World War 2 he coined the term in a letter dated 1944.

Maverick had become increasingly frustrated with the official bureaucratic terminology and wrote a memo saying, "Gobbledygook should be banned and anyone using the words activation or implementation will be shot."

Maverick later revealed the inspiration for the term was that all the jargon he heard sounded like the gobbling of turkeys: "Always gobbledygobbling and strutting with ludicrous pomposity."

The term was quickly adopted across the world and can be seen numerous times in the years after this. Still a very popular term to this day, it has inspired a children's book about a monster known as the Gobbledygook.

"Red Herring"

Meaning: a clue or piece of information which is or is intended to be misleading or distracting.

Origin: Clearly, the literal meaning of 'Red herring' is a herring which has turned red due to the smoke. The sense of the term 'Red herring' being used to mean a false or misleading piece of information seems to stem from the use of the fish itself in hunting.

The act of using herrings in laying trails for hounds for practice hunts is an old one, we can say for certain from at least the late sixteenth century, but the practice may be older. The first printed evidence is in an Elizabethan pamphlet by Thomas Nashe, 1599: "To draw on hounds to a scent, to a red herring's skin there is nothing comparable."

Such a trail was artificial and therefore false as opposed to the trail of real game in a hunt which is where the misleading angle seems to stem. There are numerous examples of red herrings being used to train hounds to follow a scent, and horses then trained to follow the hounds in the following 200 years and the term seems to have leaped to a figurative meaning of anything that is misleading sometime in the early nineteenth century.

The first printed evidence of the figurative usage comes in a piece by William Cobbett critiquing the English press, which had mistakenly reported Napoleon's defeat, 1807: "It was a mere transitory effect of the political red-herring, for, on the Saturday, the scent became as cold as a stone."

"Splitting Hairs"

Meaning: arguing or disagreeing over small, insignificant details, usually pointlessly so.

Origin: If this phrase was created today, no doubt we would be talking about splitting atoms, however, we have been 'splitting hairs' for centuries and hundreds of years ago there were not many things considered to be finer than a hair. Actually, splitting a hair would be incredibly difficult at the time and there would be little point in doing so hence the meaning of the phrase.

Before we arrive at the exact saying as we see it today, we see Shakespeare splitting hairs into fractions in his play 'Henry IV, 1597: "I'll cavil on the ninth part of a hair." Clearly, hair splitting was a thing understood at this point.

We also see the phrases 'To cut a hair', 'It's hard to split a hair' and even 'splitting straws' in the sixteenth and seventeenth century before we can see the phrase as it is now. All versions of the phrase are used figuratively so it is easy to see how we arrive with the saying soon after.

The first we see the exact phrase in print is in a translation of Gabriel D'Emillianne's 'Observations on a Journey to Naples', 1691: "Shewing himself very inventive and dexterous at splitting a hair in his way of handling Scholastick matter."

"Fresh as a Daisy"

Meaning: to be alert, energetic or enthusiastic, usually after sleep. The term can also be used to describe someone or something looking clean, tidy or well kept.

Origin: Why a daisy? Why not ice or a mint?

The clue to why the daisy is the flower of choice in this phrase is thought to lie within the name of the flower itself. The word 'daisy' is from an old English word, 'daeges eage', meaning 'days eye'.

It is thought the daisy is named so as the flower is known for opening in the morning and closing at night due to its reaction to sunlight. The name also alludes to the flowers appearance as is described in English philologist Walter William Skeats work, 1889: "The primary meaning of daeges eage is doubtless the sun, the daisy is named from its supposed likeness to the sun, the white petals being the rays, and the yellow centre the sun's sphere."

Etymologists will tell you that the daisy flower has been regarded as a 'waking flower' for centuries and it is thought this association is the reason this is the flower of choice in this phrase.

The phrase to be 'as fresh as a daisy', meaning to be healthy and full of energy, is thought to come from the conception that the daisy is never tired because it 'sleeps' regularly.

The first record of the phrase as we know it today is in 'The Town and Country Magazine', 1778: "Harry Bluster no sooner enters the room, than he gives, A yoy ho! Yoy yoy my boys, here I am, sound wind and limb, fresh as a daisy."

The phrase is clearly understood at the time for it to be in a magazine and although the origin here is a guess, it is an educated one.

"Pull One's Socks Up"

Meaning: to make an effort to improve one's work or behaviour.

Origin: Although there is no definitive origin of this phrase, there are clues in both the place and era it can be first seen. The idea of getting dressed correctly or sprucing oneself up to be ready for what may unfold is not a new one.

As a sport, cricket prides itself on its gentlemanly etiquette and pride in the way one is dressed, and it is in relation to this sport we see the term used first in print in the Scottish paper 'The Saturday Falkirk Herald', 1887: "On going to the wickets a second time, the 'muir men rigged up 42 for the loss of seven wickets. Something wrong, Jamie Morrison! How would it do to get the 2nd eleven to play your matches? Today Arthur & Co.'s Cricket Club visit the tryst ground, when surely, ye 'muir men, you will 'pull up your socks'."

Although the above piece is the first time we see the term used in the context it is today, slightly before this we see an act titled 'Pull up your socks' by the music-hall artist Will Gilbert, 1881, it is advertised as follows: "Will Gilbert, the funniest of the funny, in his great oration on the rights, wrongs, Perseverance's and backslidings of the human race, entitled 'PULL UP YOUR SOCKS'."

Two decades later, we see the following piece by a Lady Mary in 'The Pittsburgh Sunday Post', the piece talks about her visit to London, 1906: "At a bridge dinner the other evening I was startled and shocked to hear a young sprig of the nobility, who will be a marquis someday, bid a stately dowager countess of 70 to 'pull her socks up'. I learned later that 'pull your socks up' is the latest slang phrase adopted by the smart set and my informant assured me, with a touch of pride, that it was of distinctly English origin. It means 'keep cool' or 'pull yourself together'."

It is clear that the term is understood in the UK in the 1880s but not America at this time as we see several references of it in the UK and it is not understood by the lady, we also start to see the term being referenced in the early 1900s in America.

Although not conclusive, it is logical to assume that the term originated in sport, most likely cricket and that to pull your socks up meant to take pride in the way you were dressed and do things the way they should be and get on with it.

"Salt of the Earth"

Meaning: a very good, honest, worthy and reliable person or persons.

Origin: The phrase 'Salt of the earth' has its origins in the Bible, although strangely, the first recorded version of the saying predates the version of the Bible where we see the phrase printed in English.

The English version of the phrase is first seen written by English poet Geoffrey Chaucer in 'Summoners Tale', 1386: "Ye been the salt of the erthe and the savour." Chaucer is believed to have taken the lead from a Latin version of the Bible, the earliest versions of which are as old as 382AD.

The earliest English print of the Bible where we see the phrase is the King James version of the Bible, 1611: "Ye are the salt of the earth, but if the salt have lost his savour, wherewith shall it be salted? It is thenceforth good for nothing, but to be cast out, and to be trodden under foot of men."

It is believed that the 'excellent' meaning in 'the salt of the earth' was coined in reference to the value of salt. This is reflected in other old phrases too, for example, the aristocratic and powerful of the earth were 'above the salt' and valued workers were 'worth their salt'.

Not to be mixed up with 'Salting the earth', which has very negative connotations as this was the ritual of spreading salt in the soil of conquered land by the conquerors in the Middle Ages, in order to, either symbolically or literally, prevent crops from ever growing there again, thereby preventing the conquered from rebuilding.

"Make Hay Whilst the Sun Is Shining"

Meaning: take advantage of the chance to do something while conditions are good.

Origin: The idea of taking advantage of good conditions when the opportunity arises is not a new one. This idiom has its roots in farming as you may imagine and although we can trace roughly when the phrase came about, we can see similar older sayings in the Bible: "He that gathereth in summer is a wise son, but he that sleepeth in harvest is a son that causeth shame."

The first time we see the phrase in English is in John Heywood's 'A dialogue conteinyng the 179ompel in effect of all the prouerbes in the Englishe tongue', 1546: "Whan the sunne shinth make hay. Whiche is to say take time whan time cometh, lest time steale away."

Medieval farmers would be well aware of the wisdom of not leaving it too late to gather one's hay. Modern machinery and weather forecasting make haymaking reasonably quick and stress free. Tudor farmers however would have taken several days to cut, dry and gather their hay and would have had only folk rhymes such as 'red sky at night' to guide them. Forecasting the weather two or three days in advance wouldn't have been possible back then, so all the more reason for them to 'make hay while the sun shines'.

We see the phrase leap from literal to figurative roughly 100 years later and the first time we see it used in a non-farming context in print is in in Richard Head's 'Glossary of the language of thieves and beggars', 1673: "She was resolv'd to make Hay 179ompel the Sun shin'd."

"Tarred With the Same Brush"

Meaning: a person being labelled with the same faults or bad qualities as another, rightly or wrongly.

Origin: Some believe the origin of this phrase has its roots in the cruel punishment known as 'Tarring and feathering', this involved covering a person in hot pine tar littered with feathers from head to toe. The person was then ignited and ridden out of town tied to a splintery rail, beaten with sticks and stoned all the while. This public humiliation punishment was first recorded in England in 1189 and was still happening as late as the eighteenth century in America.

There is no evidence to support this theory however and etymologists believe the phrases true origins lie in sheep farming. Owners of a flock of sheep used to mark their wool all in the same place with a brush dipped in tar to distinguish them from the sheep of another flock. It is said that the red ochre was used to make the mark and that brushing sheep with tar served to protect them against ticks.

The term was transferred to likeness in human beings in the early 1800s. The first time it can be seen in print is in Sir Walter Scott's novel 'Rob Roy', 1818: "They are a' tarr'd wi' the same stick, rank Jacobites and Papists." The exact term can first be seen in William Cobbett's 'Rural Rides', 1823: "'You are all tarred with the same brush', said the sensible people of Maidstone."

"All's Fair in Love and War"

Meaning: every action taken in passion is justified and there are no rules in both love and war.

Origin: The idea behind this phrase has existed in many guises before this saying was formed. The theory of the lawless nature of both love and war and the thin line between love and hate are mentioned time and time again.

The first similar example we see in English is in John Lyly's romantic novel 'Euphues'. The anatomy of wyt'. 1578: "Anye impietie may lawfully be committed in love, which is lawlesse."

Shortly after this we see a translation in 1620 of the legendary books 'Don Quixote' written by Miguel de Cervantes, 1605: "Love and warre are all one, and as in warre it is lawful to use sleights and stratagems to overcome the enemy."

The first time we see the phrase used in its current form is in playwright William Taverner's 'The artful husband', 1717: "All advantages are fair in Love and War."

"Raining Cats and Dogs"

Meaning: a term to describe torrential rain.

Origin: after extensive research on this one I can say definitively that there IS no definitive provable origin! What I can do is debunk the theories and give you an idea of how it came about though.

Firstly, there is no meteorological recorded event where cats and dogs have rained from the skies. Much smaller water-based creatures, such as fish and frogs, have plummeted from the skies in freak storms after being carried skywards, but this is a very rare occurrence.

Secondly, I can also rubbish the story of cats and dogs living in thatched roofs being washed to the floor in heavy rain. Etymologists have looked into this and there are no records of cats or dogs residing in roofs and why on earth would they?

And finally, I can also say there is no evidence that it comes from the French word 'catadoupe', meaning waterfall.

The phrase is clearly not a literal one and the most common thought is that its origins lie in the work of poet Jonathan Swift, we see the following in his poem 'A description of a city shower', 1710: "Sweeping from butchers stalls, dung, guts and blood, drown'd puppies, stinking sprats, all drench'd in mud, dead cats and turnip tops come tumbling down the flood."

Based on places mentioned in the poem, etymologists have come to the conclusion that it is in fact floods in London that Swift is describing. It is also not considered coincidence that the very same poet is the first who has coined the phrase as we see it today nearly 30 years later in his work 'A Complete Collection of Polite and Ingenious Conversation', 1738: "I know Sir John will go, though he was sure it would rain cats and dogs."

To further cement this theory, we see the phrase being used many times following Swifts work but not before.

"In For a Penny in For a Pound"

Meaning: a person should finish what he or she has started to do even though it may be difficult or expensive.

Origin: Although the exact origin is not clearly known, etymologists believe the term probably came about in the world of gambling in the 'All in' sense of this term.

We can start to put the pieces of the puzzle together. There are examples of gambling halls existing pre-1500s in the United Kingdom. The first English pennies were introduced around 785 AD by the Anglo-Saxon King, Offa of Mercia. The pound coin first appeared in 1489, during the rule of Henry VII. Clearly gambling, pennies and pounds all needed to exist before the saying itself did so we can say for certain that the term cannot have existed before the pound did.

The first time we see the term used in print is in Edward Ravenscroft's comic play 'Canterbury Guests', 1695: "Well than, O'er shooes, o'er boots. And in for a Penny, in for a Pound."

The saying is thought to have been popularised however by none other than Charles Dickens himself. He used the term in 3 of his novels published between 1837–1840; 'Nicholas Nickleby', 'Oliver Twist' and 'The Old Curiosity Shop'.

Although the term is based on the English currency, the term is still used in America and Australia.

"Stick in the Mud"

Meaning: a person who is dull, unadventurous or resists change.

Origin: The idea of someone not willing to change their mind/opinion/views/ways have earned people the figurative labels of 'stick in the mud' for many years.

Etymologists believe the 'stick' in 'stick in the mud' has derived from the word 'stuck' as opposed to a piece of wood and that to have been stuck in the mud had the meaning of finding it difficult to change as they are literally stuck.

People have been said to be stuck in other things in times gone by, we can see historic examples of being sticks in briers, clay, mire and mud. The earliest example I can find in print is in Thomas Coopers Thesaurus, 1565: "They 185ompe accused of extortion and pillage were in muche trouble, or stacke in the bryars."

Only 'Stick in the mud' has stood the test of time and the earliest examples found are in relation to criminals not willing to change their ways. The term must have been utilised mainly for offenders not willing to change their ways as both the first examples seen in print are in relation to this –

London paper, 'The General Evening Post', November 1733: "George Fluster, alias Stick in the Mud, has made himself an Evidence, and impeached the above two Persons."

In the same paper again, December 1733: "John Anderson, Francis Ogleby, and James Baker, alias Stick in the Mud, for breaking open the House of Mr Thomas Bayner, a Silversmith, and stealing thence Plate to a great value."

It is easy to understand how the term in the years that follow transferred figuratively to someone not willing to change their ways, criminally or otherwise.

"Stick to One's Guns"

Meaning: refuse to compromise or change, despite criticism.

Origin: This term seems to have a military background in the sense of the obligation of not leaving one's post and refusing to budge regardless of potential dangers.

It is believed the term as we see it today originates from an earlier used British phrase, 'Stood to one's gun'. The first time we see this term being used in print is in James Boswell's 'Life of Johnson', 1791: "Mrs Thrale stood to her gun with great courage in defence of amorous ditties."

We can see the term at this point is being used figuratively, so presumably it has already morphed from the military term and is probably widely understood, certainly in the UK as a minimum.

Stood to one's guns is still being used in 1909 in the UK as we see in this example: "The Quakers stood to their guns, and without any resort to brute force, finally won." Although this version is used far less frequently today in the UK, with the more popular American version 'Stick to one's guns' being the phrase of choice both sides of the pond.

Though it is not certain that 'Stick to one's guns' is American in origin, all the earliest examples are based there, and we know for sure the English version is still being used in the UK when we see the American version first arrive in the States. It was first attested in the United States in 'Seven Keys to Baldpate by Earl Derr Biggers, 1913: "Stick to your guns, hold to your convictions and rights."

We can't be certain of the place of origin, although it is widely agreed to be American in the form, we see it today and it is believed this is a variant of the earlier British version. What etymologists both sides of the pond seem to agree on is that the phrase stems from military personnel being told to stand by their military post regardless of the dangers they may face. It is easy to see how the 'Refuse to be moved' stance of the saying moved from literal to figurative over time.

"Pearls of Wisdom"

Meaning: originally, this was used when something sounded very wise or helpful. More recently it has been used in an ironic sense that something is obvious and not particularly helpful.

Origin: Long known as 'The Queen of gems', pearls were once the exclusive property of the rich and powerful. There are records of ancient Egyptians and Romans using pearls as decorative items as far back as 500 BC, so it is easy to understand how a valuable piece of information began to be described as a 'pearl' in the human psyche.

In terms of the phrase itself, it is believed to be a lot more modern, and etymologists believe its origin lie in the Bible. We find the following line In the King James Bible, 1611: "No mention shall be made of coral, or of pearls, for the price of wisdom is above rubies."

We see the term 'pearls of wisdom' being used many times after this, originally in a positive light as advice that is truly precious. The term is used so frequently over the next century that it becomes a terrible cliché and at some point in the early 1800s, the term starts to be used in an ironic fashion, used when someone's advice is obvious or unhelpful.

The first example I can find in this context is in the Robert William Chambers 'The Conspirators', 1807: "Oh, how beautiful you will be!" said Osborne, looking in at the door. "My! My! All gold and feathers and precious stones and pearls of wisdom! A perfect aide-de-camp!"

"Like a Broken/Stuck Record"

Meaning: used to say that someone keeps saying the same thing over and over again.

Origin: the phrase 'like a broken record' or 'Like a stuck record' comes from the characteristics of vinyl records.

Invented in 1877 by Thomas Edison, when a vinyl record was damaged with a scratch or indent, it would 'skip' or repeat sections over and over again until someone would manually move the needle away from the bad spot.

Though we see the term being used in print from around 1900 it is thought to have been popularised by a particular record by the same name.

In 1936, we see an album of ballroom classics produced by Henry Hall and released with the name 'Broken record', the lyrics to the song 'Broken record' itself contain the following lyrics: "My Sweetheart, you're gorgeous, you're gorgeous, you're gorgeous, you're gorgeous, you're gorgeous, you're gorgeous tonight. That's a song I heard on the phonograph, the needle caught on the broken half and kept playing."

"Hogwash"

Meaning: nonsense, usually called out when something is fake.

Origin: The original meaning of 'Hogwash' was a literal one and the Oxford English dictionary defines its original meaning as 'the swill of a brewery or kitchen given to hogs'. The first quote illustrating it in this sense according to the OED is 1440.

Cooks would collect the leftovers and scraps from meals in a bucket, this mixture of food bits, including food that was rotten, was known as swill or wash and this would be fed to the pigs.

According to the OED the term started to be used when describing weak or inferior liquor some years later and the first time this can be found in print is in 1712 in a piece by London based Scottish writer John Arubthnot: "Your butler purloins your liquor, and the brewer sells you hogwash."

It is easy to understand how the word moved from waste food to poor liquor and shortly after anything that was not genuine. The current meaning of the word, as in a lie or nonsense, seems to have been popularised in American English however as we see the term used in America first in the early 1800s and then in the United Kingdom in the mid to late 1800s.

"Pushing Up Daisies"

Meaning: used to describe someone that has died.

Origin: Daisies have been associated with death long before we see the term 'Pushing up daisies' used specifically. Daisies grow easily with little to no maintenance, particularly in nutrient rich soil where a corpse may have been laid to rest. Bodies are typically sealed in coffins now however that was not always the case. Because of this it was common to see daisies growing in burial grounds.

Scottish Gaelic translator James Macpherson translated several ancient Gaelic poems in his book 'The poems of Ossian', the book was published in 1760 and within the book are descriptions of how unborn children would return to the ground as flowers.

Shortly after, in 1820, we see English Poet John Keats write the following piece: "I shall soon be laid in the quiet grave, thank God for the quiet grave, I can feel the cold earth upon me, the daisies growing over me, O for this quiet, it will be my first."

The first time we see the term used exactly as we see it today is in British poet Wilfred Owen's poem 'A Terre', 1917: "Pushing up daisies, is their creed, you know. To grain, then, go my fat, to buds my sap. For all the usefulness there is in soap."

The term became rather fashionable again with the release of the British TV show by the same name in 1984 and more recently American TV show 'Pushing daisies' in 2007.

"Silence Is Golden"

Meaning: used in circumstances where it is thought that saying nothing is preferable to speaking.

Origin: Silence has in fact long been considered laudable in religious circles and many etymologists believe this saying has its roots in ancient Egypt although there is no proof.

The first time we see the proverb is in the Judaic Biblical commentaries called the 'Midrash', roughly 600AD, which translated has the following "If speech is silvern, then silence is golden." This however wasn't translated from Old Hebrew until the 1900s so it is very possible this translation could have been influenced by already understood terminology.

We can see some similar terms in English before the translated works, in the fourteenth century in Richard Rolle's 'psalms of David', 1340, we see the following: "Discipline of silence is gold."

And shortly after in 'Wyclif's Bible', 1382, we see the following: "Silence is made in Heaven."

Later still in Spanish writer Cervantes legendary tale 'Don Quixote', 1605, we can find the following translated piece: "As Sancho says, silence is golden."

The first provable example of it written in English is from the poet Thomas Carlyle, who translated the phrase from German in 'Sartor Resartus', 1831: "Speech is silver, Silence is golden, or as I might rather express it, speech is of time, silence is of eternity."

Though we can't be certain of the origin, what we can say definitively is that 'Silence is golden' is an abbreviation of the longer saying 'Speech is silver, silence is golden' and that it is found spoken in Hebrew, Spanish and German before it is seen in English.

"Warm the Cockles of One's Heart"

Meaning: give one a comforting feeling of contentment.

Origin: There is no definitive origin for 'warm the cockles of one's heart' but there are two main theories etymologists will argue over.

The first theory is that cockles, as in the sea molluscs, have shells that can be heart shaped, particularly when the two halves of the shell are together and intact. The best example of this is 'Corculum cardissa' (Pictured here), known as the heart cockle and is a species of marine bivalve molluscs.

The second theory, and in most etymologists' opinion, the most likely theory, has its base in Biology. The heart has ventricles and cockles could be a play on this word. The cochlea is actually part of the inner ear in today's biological terms but if we look further back, we see the Latin name for the ventricles is actually 'cochleae cordis', we also see the Latin word 'Corculum', which means 'little heart'.

This may just be coincidence but many etymologists believe it is not and that this word has entered the English language via translation at some point.

Though we cannot be certain, what we can do is get some sort of idea as to the age of the saying. Though it must be older for it to be found and presumably understood in print, the first time we see the phrase written is in the work of English clergyman John Eachard, 1671: "This contrivance of his did inwardly rejoice the cockles of his heart."

"Opportunity Knocks"

Meaning: you will only have one chance to do something important or profitable.

Origin: The origin of this one is nearly impossible to find as there are so many differing opinions as to where it was conceived. What I can say is that the thought that when an opportunity arises it should be seized is a very old one indeed, ancient in fact.

In 1895, R.A.H Bickford Smith translated the work of Pubilius Syrus, the ancient Latin writer, into English and found the following phrase, dated 43 BC: "Opportunity is seldom presented, easily lost."

In the 1500s, we see another similar phrase in Medieval French writings: "Il n'est chance qui ne retourne," which translates as 'there is no opportunity which comes back again'.

We get much closer to the actual phrase we use today in Spanish writer, Cervantes, 'Don Quixote', 1605, when we see the following words when translated: "It is not fit that whilst good luck is knocking at our door, we shut it."

The first time we see the exact phrase we use today is in John Dos Passos's novel 'The 42nd Parallel', 1930: "Opportunity knocks but once at a young man's door." It is thought highly likely that the term is already in use and understood for it to be in a novel, however.

In the UK specifically, the term becomes further popularised by a popular BBC radio game show of the same name in 1949 followed by a television show running from 1987. An American show by the same name is aired in 2008.

Though we cannot be certain on the exact origin of the term as we see it today, we can say definitively the sentiment has ancient origins.

"Money Is the Root of All Evil"

Meaning: greed is the cause of a particular problem or the cause of society's problems in general.

Origin: This one was a simple one to find, although it's meaning has morphed into something slightly different today and has been abbreviated. Though the saying blames money itself in the way we use it today, originally it was a warning against lust and greed.

A very similar quote from where the current saying spawned is originally seen in the Latin Vulgate Bible 382AD, it was translated into German first by Martin Luther (1483–1546) as "Die Habsucht ist die Wurzel allen Übels," which translates as 'greed is the root of all evil'.

William Tyndale (1494–1536) was the first to translate the same text to English and it read as follows "For covetousness is the root of all evil."

The first time we see the saying involving money directly is In the King James bible, 1611: "For the love of money is the root of all evil, which while some coveted after, they have erred from the faith, and pierced themselves through with many sorrows."

In the story, St Paul is saying that money is not the problem, it's people's love or lust for money that is the problem. It's a continuing theme in the Bible that man worships false idols to his detriment.

"What's Good for the Goose Is Good for the Gander"

Meaning: if something is good for one person, it should be equally as good for another person.

Origin: Though this saying is today used in the context of what is good for one person will be just as good for another, originally it was based on it being what is good for a man is good for a woman.

Though a goose is the animal of choice in this saying we have seen other derivations of it, one example is in in John Heywood's 'A Dialogue Conteinyng the Nomber in Effect of All the Prouerbes in the Englishe Tongue', 1546: "As well for the cow as for the bull."

The first time we see the 'equality of the sexes' meaning in relation to a goose is in English writer Roger L'Estrange's translation of ancient Greek Aesop's work in 'Aesop's Fables' 1484: "Sauce for a Goose is Sauce for a Gander."

The first time we see the saying as we understand it today is in John Ray's 'A collection of English Proverbs', 1678: "That that's good sauce for a goose, is good for a gander."

As time has progressed, the 'sauce' element was lost, and the modern iteration of the phrase is born.

"Piece of Cake"

Meaning: something easily achieved.

Origin: This one is quite easy to understand in that eating a piece of cake is not an arduous task in any sense. We see the choice of cake or indeed pie or ale as a symbol of ease and pleasantry represented numerous times in history before the current saying emerges.

In Shakespeare's 'Twelfth night', 1601–1602, we see an older and now redundant phrase, 'Cakes and ale', meaning the same thing as todays saying used for the first time: "Dost thou think, because thou art virtuous, there shall be more cakes and ale."

In the 1870s, we see the term 'Cake walk' appear, a cake walk was a competition in Southern America where the best performing couples were given a piece of cake as a prize. The cake walk was more of a stroll than an energetic dance where others would judge the elegance of a couple and this term has also morphed to mean something of ease.

The first time we see the term in the figurative way we use it today is in the work of American poet Ogden Nash's 'Primrose Path', 1936: "Her picture's in the papers now, And life's a piece of cake."

"Achilles Heel"

Meaning: a weakness or vulnerable point.

Origin: This phrase comes from Greek mythology in the writings of Ancient Greek author, Homer, in his work 'Iliad'.

The story goes that Greek goddess Thetis dipped her son Achilles in the Styx, a river that was believed to be a source of incredible power and gave invulnerability. The story would tell that the only vulnerable area on Achilles body was the area she was holding him by and therefore not touched by the river.

The complication is that Homers tale didn't specifically say it was Achilles heel that was his downfall, other ancient Greek writers have said that he was felled by a shot to the elbow and even the torso by the arrow that eventually killed him. In the end, the heel was the 'weak point' story that won through from the various tales since Homers original version.

The first translation we see of Homers work into English is in 1581 by translator Arthur Hall and the first example we see in print of the term 'Achilles heel', meaning a weakness, is in Irish poet John Denham's poem 'Cooper's Hill', 1642: "Leave then, said he, the invulnerable Keel, we'll find they're feeble, like Achilles Heel."

Interestingly, Achilles is also responsible for the name of a tendon close to the heel, and we see this first named shortly after the heel is named in English. The first example found in print of the tendon being named so is in Flemish anatomist Philip Verheyen's writing 'Corporis Humani Anatomia', 1693: describing the tendon as 'The cord of Achilles'.

"A Sight for Sore Eyes"

Meaning: a person or thing that one is extremely pleased or relieved to see.

Origin: The reference to 'sore' in this saying is not that of being in pain but of being upset, in the same context we state something is upsetting or distressing when we say something is a 'sore point'.

We can definitively locate the origin of this one and it is sits with English Author, Jonathan Swift's story 'Polite conversation', 1738: "The Sight of you is good for sore Eyes." Swift is most well-known for his book 'Gulliver's Travels'.

Over time the phrase becomes abbreviated to just 'A sight for sore eyes' and the first time we can see this in print is in a piece by William Hazlitt in 'New Monthly Magazine', 1826: "He should act in tragedy and comedy, what a sight for sore eyes that would be!"

"At Loggerheads"

Meaning: in or into a state of quarrelsome disagreement.

Origin: 'Loggerheads' is the name of three small towns in the UK, in Staffordshire, Lancashire and Mold. 'Loggerhead' is also the name of a species of both a turtle and a bird. None of these are the origin, and although locals in the Towns I mentioned will stake a claim to it, there is literally no evidence to support this.

Originally, a 'Loggerhead' was a comedic reference to a stupid person, in the way we might say 'Blockhead' now. The first example of this is in Shakespeare's 'Love's Labour's Lost', 1588: "Ah you whoreson logger-head, you were borne to doe me shame."

The Shakespeare reference is not thought to be the origin either as the meaning is not the same today, as in the quarrel meaning. Perhaps it did influence the name of the seventeenth century tool however by the same name. A loggerhead is recorded as 'an iron instrument with a long handle used for melting pitch and for heating liquids'.

Though not definitive, etymologists find it likely that the use of these tools as weapons was what was being referred to when rivals were first said to be 'at loggerheads'.

The first known use of the phrase in print is in Francis Kirkman's, 'The English Rogue', 1680: "They frequently 200ompel200'd about their Sicilian wenches, and indeed they seem to be worth going to Logger-heads for."

"A Dime a Dozen"

Meaning: so plentiful as to be valueless.

Origin: The dime was first minted in 1796. In the mid-1800s, many goods such as eggs or apples can be seen in newspaper advertisements with the branding 'a dime a dozen' in the United States. A phrase that began as a way to tout good value for the money evolved into a phrase that means something nearly worthless by virtue of its commonness and easy availability.

The first example I can find in print is in the 'Galveston Daily News' 1866: "The San Antonio Ledger says the city is well stocked with peaches at a dime a dozen."

The phrase becomes so popular in the late 1800s that it begins to be used in a figurative way meaning anything that is plentiful or common. The first figurative example I can find is in the 'Northern Miner' newspaper, 1931: "As for the other clowns, Schaof, Baer, Paulino, Risko and Campolo, they're nothing but dime a dozen fighters."

'A dime a dozen' clearly originates in America due to the currency involved in the phrase however etymologists believe its origins could lie with the UK currency, the penny.

In the UK, the phrase 'ten a penny' is more common and we see offers advertised in this way earlier than the American version. One famous example of the deal involved in a penny is in the nursery rhyme 'Hot cross buns' which is first recorded in 'Poor man's almanac' in 1733, although the nursery rhyme states, "One a penny, two a penny, hot cross buns," not ten a penny. Advertisements for 'Ten a penny' can be seen shortly after this.

It is very possible the American version is a translation of the English version, though there is no definitive proof of this.

"In Layman's Terms"

Meaning: explaining a complicated piece of information in brief, simplified or easy to understand words.

Origin: According to the Oxford English Dictionary 'Layman' was not one individual but actually a reference to a group of followers of a religion but not educated enough to be part of the clergy itself.

The term is very old indeed and is a morph of two words, 'Lay' and 'Man', as opposed to an individual named 'Layman'.

The etymologists will tell you Ancient Greeks used the term 'Laos' first which simply meant 'people', this was followed by the Latin word 'Laicus' which meant the same thing. In 1303, we see the term 'Lai' in French first used and in 1338 we see 'Lay' first used in English, both terms are used to describe common people, or in today's terms, uneducated people.

In all early instances of the terms 'lay' or 'layman' being referenced it is used to describe words the followers would understand that were not as steeped in religion as the clergymen themselves.

The term 'Layman's terms' continued to be used in religious circles but at some point in the seventeenth and eighteenth centuries, it started to be used in both medical and legal circles as a way of breaking things down for the uneducated as both profession's used complex terminology.

It is impossible to give a conclusive date for the birth of the term as we see it today but etymologists are confident this is how the term came to be. The term is now used widely in all professions where jargon may not be understood by those uneducated in a particular profession.

"Sitting Duck"

Meaning: a person or thing that is easy to hit, attack or trick.

Origin: This phrase comes, unsurprisingly, from hunting. A sitting duck is easy prey for a hunter, some ducks, such as the mallard are known as 'dabbling ducks' which means they look for their food near the water's surface.

These ducks often float, or 'sit' on top of the water as they search for food. Sitting ducks are especially vulnerable to hunters because they are out in the open with no protection and are much easier targets than when they are airborne.

It is easy to see how the term has come to be used figuratively for anything that was an easy victim, human or otherwise and the first time the term can seen in this way is in 'The Courier-Mail', 1940: "The German airmen are shooting 'sitting ducks', yet, night and day, from low and high altitudes, they have succeeded only in hitting residential districts."

The term is clearly already being used figuratively for it to be in a newspaper and was being used literally much earlier.

The term became popularised in the late twentieth century by the famous poster art by Michael Bedard in 1977 (pictured below) a film in 1980, popular children's book in 1998 and TV show in 2001 all with the name 'Siting duck'.

Now I feel I have all my ducks in a row...another popular idiom and frustratingly one I can't get to the bottom of!

"Bite the Dust"

Meaning: said when someone is killed or fails at something.

Origin: This one is easy to understand, if someone is killed and falls to their fate, they may well finish life with whatever is on the floor in their face. Although this one is often associated with the era of the Wild West in America, 1865–95, it is in fact much older.

Translated in the nineteenth century by Samuel Butler, the epic poem 'The Iliad', written by Ancient Greek writer Homer, around 700 BC, we see the following: "Grant that my sword may pierce the shirt of Hector about his heart, and that full many of his comrades may bite the dust as they fall dying round him."

We also see an English variant and redundant phrase in the 'king James Bible', 1611: "They that dwell in the wilderness shall bow before him and his enemies shall lick the dust."

The earliest citation of the term in its exactity is found in 'Adventures of Gil Blas of Santillane' by the Scottish author Tobias Smollett, 1750: "We made two of them bite the dust, and the others betake themselves to flight."

Of course, one of the reasons the phrase has stayed mainstream is the hit song 'Another one bites the dust' recorded by Queen in 1980.

"One's Number Is Up"

Meaning: used when someone is doomed to die or suffer some other disaster or setback.

Origin: Though not definitive, etymologists believe this phrase has its roots in the Bible. There are a number of passages in different stories relating to counting the number of days one has to live and it is believed that this is where the term has spawned.

Although there are much older versions of the bible they don't always translate directly into English and the first time we can see a similar term being used in English is in the 'King James Bible', in 'The Book of Job' 1611: "Knowest thou it, because thou wast then born? Or because the number of thy days is great?"

Much later in the nineteenth century, we see another very similar term being used by the U.S Army describing a dead soldier as 'losing his mess number'. and at a similar time we see the UK's Royal navy describing a drowned soldier as losing 'the number of his mess'. In Military terms, a mess is an area where a soldier socialises or lives, for example area on a ships deck. Again, though not definitive it is believed this term stemmed from the preaching's in the Bible.

"Short Shrift"

Meaning: rapid and unsympathetic dismissal.

Origin: The word 'Shrive' is now an almost redundant word but was commonly used in medieval times when a confessor was near to death, a priest would 'shrive' them by imposing a penance called a 'shrift', in order to provide absolution.

Shrove Tuesday, now often referred to as Pancake Day, derives from shriving, originally a day when people were shriven and more recently a day when we toss pancakes.

The first known use of 'short shrift' in print relates to the history of the British monarchy. Following the death of Edward IV in 1483, the Duke of Gloucester was appointed Lord Protector of England. He accused Lord Hastings of plotting against him and arranged for him to be executed. Hastings was allowed only a 'short shrift' as Gloucester was anxious to get his dinner.

An account of this story was printed almost a hundred years later by the English writer Raphael Holinshed in The Chronicles of England, 1577: "Lorde Chamberlaine, 206omp the Protectour hade speede and shrine him apace, for by Saint Paule I will not to dinner till I see thy head off. It mattered not to him to aske why, but made a short shrift for a longer would not be suffered, the Protector made so much hast to dinner."

Shakespeare himself had undoubtedly read the Chronicles before he wrote 'Richard III', first performed in 1594, as his account of the events differ little from Holinshed's:

GLOUCESTER: "Off with his head! Now, by Saint Paul I swear, I will not dine until I see the same."

RATCLIFF: "Dispatch, my lord Hastings, the duke would be at dinner, make a short shrift, he longs to see your head."

We don't see 'short shrift' appear in America until much later and the first I can find it in print is from the 'Adams Sentinel', 1841: "It was believed that a short shrift and a speedy doom would be awarded to the guilty."

"Rule of Thumb"

Meaning: a broadly accurate guide or principle, based on experience or practice rather than theory.

Origin: The popular theory in the UK is that 'rule of thumb' derived from a law that a man may beat his wife with a stick so long as it was no thicker than his thumb.

I can dispel this theory completely; the story goes that Judge Sir Francis Buller made a legal ruling in 1782 that a man may beat his wife with such a stick. Although Buller was notoriously harsh in his rulings there is nothing to support this and it is theorised that people at the time made him out to be worse than he actually was.

Nearly 100 years later, we see Edward Foss, in his work 'The Judges of England', 1870, wrote that, despite a searching investigation into the workings of Buller: "No substantial evidence has been found that he ever expressed so ungallant an opinion."

Further evidence that this story is not true is that firstly, there is no association of the phrase being used in the context of domestic violence until as late as the 1970s, and secondly, that the phrase can be seen in print well before Buller was even born.

The first time we see the phrase in print appears in a sermon given by the English puritan James Durham in 'Heaven Upon Earth', 1658: "Many profest Christians are like to foolish builders, who build by guess, and by rule of thumb and not by Square and Rule."

The origin of the phrase remains unknown. It is thought likely that it refers to one of the numerous ways that thumbs have been used over time to estimate things, judging the alignment or distance of an object by holding the thumb in one's eye line and this is certainly what this early print would suggest.

"Wet Behind the Ears"

Meaning: lacking experience or immature.

Origin: This idiom is a fairly logical one and is an allusion to the inexperience of a baby, as when they are born, they enter the world covered in amniotic fluid from the womb and the last area to be dried is often behind the ears.

The saying itself is relatively new in English however it can be found centuries before in German: "*Nass hinter den Ohren*," meaning 'wet behind the ears' can be found in German first in 1642.

Before the idiom is common language in English, we see further evidence that the term is of German origin in the work of American translator Oliver Oldschool translating a German book in Philadelphia paper 'The Portfolio', 1802: "Young Americans are for the most part, excessively silly company, the well-educated and travelled persons excepted. The French call such inexperienced uneducated boys, green creoles, (des 208ompel208 verts,) as in German we usually say of such a person, 'He is not yet dry behind the ears'."

The saying is seen in print (where not translated) in both English and French around the same time. The earliest citation of it in English is seen in New Hampshire paper 'The Portsmouth Daily Times' in 1911: "There is not much in the matter so far as the organ is concerned except it is so new that it is wet behind the ears yet." And in French paper 'Société des traditions' 1912, 'phrase *mouillé derrière les oreilles*' meaning 'wet behind the ears'.

We also see in America in the early twentieth century the term 'dry behind the ears' being used which means 'experienced' but this term was and is far less common.

What we can say fairly definitively is that the 'wet' in question is almost certainly amniotic fluid and that the term is almost certainly of German origin as it appears in print almost 200 years before it is seen in other languages.

"Going For Broke"

Meaning: risking everything to reap substantial reward.

Origin: This idiom comes from the world of gambling and specifically originally is associated with the dice game 'Craps'. This game might be played at casinos and those playing have the option of wagering everything on a single dice roll. This is a risky move however, because a bad roll could result in them losing all of their money and leave them 'broke'.

The term 'Broke' according to the Oxford English Dictionary has been used to mean 'bankrupt' since the late seventeenth century but the term 'Going for broke' is much more recent. The term is thought to have been used specifically in casinos and did not start to be used figuratively for other risks until later.

The first time the phrase can be seen used fig,uratively is in 'The Richmond River Herald and Northern Districts Advertiser', 1935: "They decided to do things properly, and their favourite contractor was told to go for broke, as the saying is." Presumably, the term is already in use for it to be understood in print at this time.

The term is thought to have been popularised by the 1951 war movie 'Going for broke'.

"Mind One's P's and Q's"

Meaning: used to warn someone to behave well and avoid giving offence.

Origin: There is no definitive origin for this one however I can offer you the main theories and add some fact so you can make your own mind up.

The first popular theory is that 'P's & Q's' is an abbreviation of 'Please's and thank-you's' with the Q representing the similar sounding end of 'Thank-you's'. This one is mentioned a few times when I researched it but has literally no evidence to support it other than that it would fit with the way we still use it today.

The second popular theory is from the world of seventeenth century English pubs and taverns. Pints and quarts were measurements of alcohol, and a theory is that bartenders would keep watch on the pints and quarts and would need to be careful not to mix them up on their tallies for stock and ordering processes. Again, there is nothing to support this other than people arguing online that this is their preferred version of origin.

The third theory, and in my opinion the most likely theory, has some evidence to support it and this version of events is most favoured by the Oxford English Dictionary who reviewed the phrase in 2007.

The letters 'p' and 'q' in lower case are very similar in that they are exact mirror images of each other in lower case in the same sense as the letters 'b' and 'd'. The theory on this one is that it is to help people learning to write to be grammatically correct.

To support this theory, we see a poem written by Charles Churchill in 1763: "On all occasions next the chair, He stands for service of the Mayor, And to instruct him how to use, His A's and B's, and P's and Q's."

One hundred years later, we still see reminders of the importance of getting the letters the correct way round as part of the education system in W.D Henkle's 'Educational Notes and Queries', 1876: "Note your p's and q's, because the distinction of majuscule P and Q does not pose a problem."

This third theory (And there are many other less common theories) seems the most likely based on the evidence and the importance of saying the right thing grammatically which has a similar meaning to the phrase in the way it is used today, to say the right thing in order to avoid offence. We cannot be absolutely certain of this however so I will leave you to decide.

"Under the Thumb"

Meaning: under someone's control or influence.

Origin: One very popular theory for this phrase is from the world of falconry, bird handlers can use their thumbs to trap a bird and stop it flying away, there is literally no evidence to back this theory, nor is it mentioned in this context historically.

Where we can see the phrase being used throughout history is in reference to someone in power that has control over groups of people, for example, a King or Lord exercising control over their subjects.

The earliest example found of the phrase is in reference to this in 'The life and posthumous works of Arthur Maynwarning' written by the English politician of the same name, 1715: "The French King having them under his Thumb, 211ompel'd them to go at his Pace."

Clearly the phrase is well known enough to be abbreviated as we see the word 'Thumbing' being used to describe something with the same meaning over 100 years later in James Halliwell's 'Dictionary of archaic and provincial words', 1847: "Thumbing: A Nottingham phrase, used to describe that species of intimidation practised by masters on their servants when the latter are compelled to vote as their employers please."

The phrase still means the same today as it did over 300 years ago in the sense of someone having control over another. Over time, the phrase has been watered down somewhat and is quite often used as a tongue in cheek statement that one's partner or lover has control over them.

In 1966, we also see the release of the Rolling Stones hit single 'Under my thumb' which popularised the phrase for the modern generation.

"You're Nicked"

Meaning: arrested or caught by the authorities, usually used in context with the police.

It would appear the verb 'Nick' has many meanings, other than my name of course!

Origin: We first see it appear around 1530, meaning to put a notch in something for measurement, a nick was a small measurement and this is why we see the phrase 'In the nick of time' meaning by a fine margin but this is clearly not in relation to being arrested or the prison meaning.

'Nick' is also used in the sense of stealing something as well as arresting someone, the first time we see it being used in the context of 'taking away' is in the work of English dramatist George Whetstone, 1576: "I neuer nickt the poorest of his pay, but if hee lackt, hee had before his day."

We see the verb being used many times in the following years in the sense of tricking, cheating or defrauding someone. The point being, the verb is used to mean taking something away, which is why it is believed 'you're nicked' is used in the context of taking a criminal away and placing them in custody.

The first time we see it used in this context is in a play by John Fletcher and Philip Massinger called 'The Propetess'. 1640: "We must be sometimes wittie, to nick a knave." A 'Knave' meant a dishonest or unscrupulous man.

So we know roughly how long the term has been used, but why 'Nick'?, nobody knows for sure but the most popular theory is that it may be an abbreviation of the word 'iniquity' meaning immoral or grossly unfair behaviour, I'll let you decide!

"More Haste Less Speed"

Meaning: trying to do something quickly may lead to mistakes and take longer in the end.

Origin: There are numerous similar examples of this phrase throughout history and the notion of haste being counterproductive can be traced back to at least Jesus Ben Sirach's apocryphal 'Book of Wisdom', 190BC, the translated work reads as follows: "There is one that 214umber and laboureth, and maketh haste, and is so much the more behind."

The first time we see something very similar without translation is in the legendary English poet Geoffrey Chaucer's work 'Canterbury tales', 1387: "In wikked haste is not profit."

Legendary playwright and poet John Heywood also had a similar version in 'A Dialogue conteinyng the 214umber in effect of all the Prouerbes in the Englishe tongue', 1546: "Moste tymes he seeth, the more haste the lesse spede."

Finally, acclaimed English naturalist John Ray (1627–1705) can be seen to make a longer version of the phrase in his work 'A collection of English proverbs', this was published in 1768 after his death: "'Haste makes waste, and waste makes want, and want makes strife between the goodman and his wife."

What we can say is that the advice to take one's time over a task in order to avoid errors is ancient advice, backed up by virtually every classic writer and poet... I really hope I haven't made any typos!

"You Reap What You Sow"

Meaning: your deeds, good or bad, will repay you in kind.

Origin: The idea of karma, meaning the sum of a person's actions now having an effect on their fate in the future, is not a new one.

The word 'Karma' itself is from the word 'Karman' which is native to the language 'Sanskrit' which was spoken in ancient South Asia roughly between 1500 to 500 BC in the area we now know as India. The word meant back then what it does today.

We can see ancient translations of the phrase 'You reap what you sow' in very old translated Bibles, the oldest translation being the 'Codex Vaticanus' Latin Bible wrote around 300AD, translated we see: "As ye sow, so shall ye reap."

The first time we see the phrase in English as we understand it now is from the 'King James Bible' in the story 'Galatians' 1611: "God is not mocked, for Whatsoever a man soweth, that shall he also reap."

The phrase is mentioned in several Biblical stories as a lesson on karma, but this is the first version, and it is easy to understand why we may figuratively use the sowing of seeds well in order to garner a good crop.

"Cut Me Some Slack"

Meaning: allow someone some leeway in their conduct.

Origin: The origin of this one is a process rather than a definitive start date. According to the Oxford English Dictionary 'Slack' has been used as early as 897AD to mean 'idle' or 'lazy', legendary English writer Geoffrey Chaucer described the word 'slack' as 'loose, not taught' in 1386.

The specific terms 'Cut' or 'Give me some slack' have nautical origins, sailing involves a lot of ropes to control a ship and a 'Slack' rope may need tightening or would allow movement on a sail. It is easy to see how the figurative way the term is used today, meaning someone needing some leeway, could originate from the loosening of a tight rope to allow movement.

We can see similar terminology used in Royal Navy Officer William Henry Smyth's 'The sailors word book', printed two years after his death in 1867: "'Slack' is otherwise considered a bad thing. To be 'slack in stays' means your ship was slow in going about or applied to a lazy man. A 'slack helm' means your ship is 'too much by the stern', which carries the helm a-lee."

Googles 'Ngram viewer' which measures how frequently words and phrases are used to give an indication of the age of something dates 'give him some slack' being used from 1900 and 'cut him some slack' as late as 1960, so although the origin may lie in sailing, the figurative term was not being used until quite recently.

We see other similar examples in the modern era such as 'Slack off' or 'slacker' being used in the lazy or loose context.

"Don't Put All Your Eggs in One Basket"

Meaning: one should not concentrate all efforts and resources in one area as one could lose everything.

Origin: This one is a relatively simple one in that it is obvious that it is a big risk to make everything dependent on one thing. One shouldn't put all one's resources into one thing or depend on success from a single plan as metaphorically should the basket fall, all one's eggs will break.

The question with this one is more a case of the age of the idiom.

This one has a definitive 'first in print' and this is another that sits at the door of legendary Spanish writer Miguel de Cervantes in his book 'Don Quixote', 1605, the following translated piece can be found: "Tis the part of wise man to keep himself today for tomorrow, and not venture all his eggs in one basket."

Shortly after Cervantes work, we see numerous similar examples, Italian writer Giovanni Torriano moved to England and translated many Spanish and Italian proverbs into English, in 1666 he converted an Italian proverb "Venture not all in one bottom."

English writer Samuel Palmer wrote in his book 'Moral Essays on proverbs', 1710: "Don't venture all your Eggs in One Basket."

There are many similar Biblical terms we see used throughout history, warning of the dangers of gambling on one sole endeavour, and although we cannot be 100% certain of the origin what we can say is that the origin of the term specifically is highly likely to be Spanish and that this is another we can thank Cervantes masterful work for.

"The Tables Have Been Turned"

Meaning: reverse the positions of adversaries. Used most commonly when the weaker position subsequently becomes dominant.

Origin: Some people believe this saying is in relation to a story in the Bible of Jesus flipping moneychanger tables however there is no evidence to support this as the origin of the phrase.

Etymologists agree that the tables in question here are those that board games are played on and the specific game thought to be the origin of the saying is backgammon. The phrase 'turn the tables' derives from these games and from the practise of reversing the board so that players play from their opponent's previous position.

Games within the family of backgammon have been played as far back as 5000 years ago and have been recorded in Mesopotamia and Persia, the saying however is more recent and the first time the saying can be seen correlates with the birth of backgammon rules as we see them today, seventeenth century England.

Though the phrase itself may be slightly older in the specific context of board games, the first time we see the term 'Turn tables' being used figuratively is in playwright George Chapman's 'The widdowes teares', 1612: "You doe well, sir, to take your pleasure of me, I may turne tables with you 'ere long."

The next example we see is in Robert Sanderson's 'XII sermons', 1634: "Whosoever thou art that dost another wrong, do but turn the tables: imagine thy neighbour were now playing thy game, and thou his."

We see numerous examples of the phrase being used from this time onwards.

"Running Around Like a
Blue Arse Fly"

Meaning: used to describe someone engaged in constant, frantic activity or movement.

Origin: Though I cannot be definitive on the origin of this one, I can make an educated guess on where it spawned.

First of all, the fly in question is the Calliphora vomitoria, less formally known as the blue bottle because of its metallic blue colour, hence the 'Blue arse' in question.

The phrase 'like a blue arse fly' is thought to be a Military term, the phrase can be seen used at points by all the services in the armed forces, but the first example is in the Navy. The earliest example is first recorded in an article written by Royal Navy Officer Claude Lionel Cumberledge for magazine 'Master Mariner' 1936: "Mani, who was here, there and everywhere, working like a trojan and dancing about like a blue-arsed fly in a strange roundhouse."

Further evidence that it is specifically a Naval term is that the most famous protagonist to use the term is The Duke of Edinburgh himself, Prince Philip, who served in the Royal Navy. Although he didn't invent the term, he famously describes the press trying to get pictures of the Royal Family as 'running round like a blue arsed fly' in 1970. The quote was one of many amusing quotes Prince Philip has said but this specific quote is deemed to have made the saying more mainstream.

But the question is why this fly? What I can tell you is that the blue bottle fly (Calliphora vomitoria), is faster than the normal house fly (musca domestica). The blue bottle travels at 6.8mph versus the 4.5mph a house fly travels and therefore potentially they 'run around' a little faster.

To further back up the Navy origin theory, the blue bottle fly's Pupae are considerably smaller than the maggot and are dark brown in colour and less easy to detect so could potentially not be spotted when a ship set off for sail.

"The Die Is Cast"

Meaning: an event has happened, or a decision has been taken that cannot be changed.

Origin: The 'die' here is the singular of dice and the cast here means thrown. So, the phrase means the dice have been thrown and therefore cannot be changed.

Interestingly, the first dice were actually worked knuckle bones of sheep, goats or cows. The more refined cube shape with dots representing numbers can first be found in the area we now know as Pakistan. Archeologists have found cube dice like this when looking into ancient ruins of the Indus Valley civilisation in the City of Mohenjo-Daro. They are dated between 2500–1900BC making dice as we know them know 4000 years old.

The phrase itself is thought to have come from Julius Caesar himself. The Latin writings of Gaius Suetonius Tranquillus (69–122AD) quote Julius Caesar saying, "*Iacta alea est,*" which translates as 'the dice have been thrown' before crossing the Rubicon River into Italy from Gaul this invading his own country and starting a civil war. Caesar died 100 years before Suetonis was born however so the quote cannot be certain, what is certain is that it was at least stated nearly 2000 years ago.

We don't see the exact quote in English until much much later, the first it can be seen in print is in Sir Thomas Herbert's 'A relation of some yeares travaile begunne into Afrique and the Greater Asia', 1634: "Aiijb, is the die cast, must at this one throw all thou hast gaind be lost?"

Below are some ancient bone dice used by the Romans, the kind Caesar himself will have used.